DE
CON
STRUC
TING

DECONSTRUCTING

and

Reconstructing Sentences

Core Principles of Grammar and Style: A Workshop

Joseph Gansrow, PhD

TATE PUBLISHING
AND ENTERPRISES, LLC

Published by Tate Publishing & Enterprises, LLC
127 E. Trade Center Terrace | Mustang, Oklahoma 73064 USA
1.888.361.9473 | www.tatepublishing.com

Tate Publishing is committed to excellence in the publishing industry. The company reflects the philosophy established by the founders, based on Psalm 68:11,
"The Lord gave the word and great was the company of those who published it."

Book design copyright © 2015 by Tate Publishing, LLC. All rights reserved.
Cover design by Nikolai Purpura
Interior design by Honeylette Pino

Published in the United States of America

ISBN: 978-1-63449-934-7
1. Language Arts & Disciplines / Grammar & Punctuation
2. Language Arts & Disciplines / Composition & Creative Writing
15.05.07

ACKNOWLEDGMENTS

Many people contributed to this book. Thanks to my students, especially those at Jericho High School, Suffolk County Community College, and those students I tutored, whose drafts, conferences, questions, and feedback shaped the content of the book. A special thanks to Spencer Lundy for experimenting with and providing feedback on many of the exercises. Thank you to all of my students for allowing me to try and err with the drafts of the book and for courageously and insightfully pointing out the many embarrassing errors. Thanks to the creative, imaginative, and professional staff at Tate for assembly and guidance. Thanks to my teachers, especially Dr. Bishop Hunt and Dr. Terrence Bowers, the most devoted and encouraging teachers I ever had. My brother Jim—thanks for introducing me to theories about core knowledge. Michael Hartnett, a generous editor, a gentle motivator, and dear friend—thank you for scrutinizing the manuscript. Thank you, Celeste Desario, for reading early drafts, providing feedback about layout, and for supporting me always. My wife, a supportive and thoughtful critic—thank you for serving as critical ear and scrutinizing eye, and always a tender heart. And to my children—thank you for your immortal smiles and passion for all that's innocent and fun.

CONTENTS

PART 3 STRUCTURE AND STYLE OF
SENTENCES AND PARAGRAPHS

PART 4 CLARITY, COHESION, AND CREATIVITY
IN TITLES, OPENINGS, AND CONCLUSIONS

PART 5 TECHNICAL ASPECTS OF COMPOSITIONS

Preface

CAN WE AND SHOULD WE CREATE A COMMON CORE?

In a *New York Times* editorial, Stanley Fish created a stir when he asked "What should colleges teach?" Frustrated by his students' inability to write a "clean sentence in English," (and it should be noted these students were also *instructors* in his college's composition program), Fish wanted to know what composition courses at his college were actually teaching students. During his research, he found that writing classes *don't* often teach writing; instead, they are too preoccupied with teaching important but distracting non-writing content, such as ideas about the environment, gender, and race. In his view, this preoccupation with non-compositional content contributes to the poor quality of writing instruction and writing that many of us (students and teachers) have also observed.

Fish does not claim that social issues such as gender and race aren't important; however, when composition instructors require students to devote time inside and outside the classroom to reading about those topics, they sacrifice instruction in writing concepts such as sentence variety, transitions, and argument, to instruction in reading. More than twenty years ago, Maxine Hairston, in her essay "Diversity, Ideology, and Teaching Writing," observed that too many writing courses seem grounded in "the social goals of the teacher" and place those needs "before the educational needs of the student." Fish and Hairston are right about the amount of time students spend on non-compositional content, and they raise important questions that any teacher and community should ask about curricular objectives: What are the educational needs of students in English and composition classes? How can we discover what writing students need to learn and how to improve their competency? What should students learn about writing and when should they learn it?

In composition courses at my college, I assign a research paper that asks students to evaluate their experiences as writing students. Those papers substantiate Fish and Hairston's findings since most students describe a composition lineage that is devoid of…composition! The most serious criticism students have of their composition education is that if they wrote at all during middle school and high school, they wrote only in English class. Since the foundation of the middle school and high school English curriculum is reading-based, students spend most of their time *talking* about books, not *writing* about them. Classroom work focuses primarily on themes and literary techniques, but very rarely on the rhetorical techniques and stylistic decisions of the writer. There is so much talking about others' writing and so little writing. When students do get a writing assignment, it's rare, because teachers often spend weeks, if not months, teaching *one* book before providing students with a writing assignment. Those writing assignments usually afford little practice with what students want and need most from composition instruction—opportunities to experiment with sentence and paragraph forms, methods for opening and closing a piece of writing, and techniques for transitioning and organizing an essay. This reading-based model, which prevents students from writing until they've read a text, privileges reading over writing and effectively reduces opportunities for students to write and receive feedback on their writing. This model may also serve as the one that future composition instructors emulate when they themselves become teachers in programs such as Fish's and at schools and colleges nation-wide.

Why don't students write anymore? One reason they don't is very unflattering to the education profession. The dirty little secret about teaching is that evaluating writing is the most labor intensive and intellectually demanding part of the job. It's much easier to lecture about a topic than it is to scrutinize dozens of compositions and provide meaningful feedback on them. Our students, however, would be better served if they wrote more frequently and received regular, timely feedback on their writing. Reading intensive and socially conscious writing instructors should recognize that students' writing is the most important and useful text in the classroom. Students, as Hairston points point, offer the tapestry of diversity that instructors need. Their writing can more often serve as the text with which to learn not only composition skills, but also critical thinking skills. By sharing and responding to each other's writing, students can learn what we want them to learn about intellectual and cultural diversity, and about civility and humanity in general.

But merely writing and receiving feedback is not sufficient for a writer's development. Writers should have the ability to understand their writing at the most fundamental level. Writers need to be able break down their sentences into component parts so that they can dissect and improve their writing. An underlying assumption of this book is that knowledge of the parts and functions of sentence parts will improve competency in writing. If students know some basics about sentence anatomy (parts) and physiology (functions), they will be more inclined to write and read better. Unfortunately, it seems that too many writing students don't learn about the functions of the words they use. In fact, most can't even identify the parts (adjective, adverb, noun), let alone explain their basic functions.

If students know the anatomy and physiology of sentences, they can improve from draft to draft in a manner very similar to the way professional athletes improve from game to game. Equipped with such knowledge of sentence parts, writers can review their writing, as athletes do game footage, and evaluate what they did, why, the effects, and, most importantly, they'll be capable of producing different and ultimately more effective ways of conveying their ideas. Basketball players watch footage of their performance to improve. In the film room, Player X sees that he regularly takes long jump shots with lots of time remaining on the twenty-four-second shot clock. Very often, he misses those shots. His team tends to lose games in which he frequently takes those types of shots. The player then works with his coach on learning techniques for evaluating and improving his performance. Instead of shooting a long jump shot, he practices faking the shot and dribbling closer to the basket for a closer, more makeable shot. He also practices driving toward the basket and passing to a teammate who is open and in position to take a more makeable shot.

Composition students should be equipped with the analogous knowledge needed to evaluate their writing;

they should be able to ask themselves, "What did I do and what options do I have to do it better?" They should be able to deconstruct a paragraph the way a player deconstructs game tape, identifying, for example, whether sentences rely too much on helping verbs or the verb to be or if sentences can more precisely convey meaning to their readers. Students can use that knowledge of sentence parts to make transformative and very meaningful revisions to their writing in a way that goes well beyond mechanical or cosmetic changes. Many students haven't been taught the composition equivalent of dribbling, yet we send them to compete in collegiate basketball!

In *A Community of Writers*, Peter Elbow and Pat Belanoff describe a sports-related approach to revision as a metacognitive replay. This approach, in which students think about and write about what they wrote, is critical for success in writing, but many composition instructors, including Belanoff and Elbow, don't advocate equipping students with the knowledge they need to create a replay. I was trained in composition theory by proponents of theories espoused by Elbow and Belanoff, whose principles of composition were inculcated by my instructors at Stony Brook University. (Belanoff and Elbow both taught at Stony Brook shortly before I enrolled.) In fact, *A Community of Writers* was a required textbook when I enrolled in the Practicum in Teaching Writing, a course designed to teach graduate students how to teach composition. Elbow and Belanoff assume that the replay is possible without knowledge of sentence anatomy and physiology, and it is, but the footage is very grainy when students don't know their grammar. Their approach *restricts* what students can see in a replay of their writing and *limits* what they can do when revising their writing. By failing to equip students with the vocabulary (adverb, adjective, clause, for example) of sentence parts and the knowledge of how those parts function (describe verbs, modify nouns, subordinate information), writing instructors obstruct students' vision and circumscribe their revision potential.

But what should students learn about sentence parts and their functions, and how should they learn it? Rei Noguchi's *Grammar and the Teaching of Writing* makes a compelling case for teaching grammar more productively by teaching grammar as "a tool for writing improvement," and not in vacuo. For Noguchi, grammar should only be taught when grammar and writing overlap. His assumption is that grammar and writing overlap in very few places, and that knowledge of grammar "cannot help, at least not directly" writers seeking to improve their content. Although Noguchi asks important pedagogical questions about what we teach, why we teach it, and how we can teach writing better, I disagree with his assumptions and his answers. We should empower students with the knowledge of the *vocabulary and functions of major sentence parts*; we should provide students with *opportunities to experiment* with those parts of sentences; we should offer them feedback on their decisions and teach students how to provide feedback to each other about their sentences.

This book assumes that if we teach students the functions of rudimentary sentence types and sentence parts so that they can deconstruct and reconstruct their sentences, they can understand their writing from what Noguchi calls a "reader-based perspective rather than from a writer-based one." When students think like readers (asking, for example, *Will readers know what I mean? Am I boring them? Does this word convey what I want? Are there other words that can better achieve my purposes? Is this word even necessary?*), they will writer better. But until students learn some of the basic vocabulary and functions of sentence parts, they won't be able to harness the imagination, sympathy, or knowledge necessary to think critically, like readers.

In order to write from a reader's perspective, writing instructors must, as unpalatable as it seems, indulge in some prescriptive approaches to teaching writing. As objectionable as initiatives such as the Common Core are, at least they have compelled educators to think about what content students need to learn and when they need to learn it. Since it's easier for most readers of our writing—colleagues, human resources departments, family—to recognize a grammatical error than a rhetorical one, it is important for students to be competent with the fundamental aspects of grammar. Furthermore, grammatical competency and rhetorical effectiveness are not mutually exclusive; in fact, they are far more connected than some of us think. If writers don't know the major rules and can't work within the currently acceptable forms, then they will probably not succeed academically or professionally. The book's underlying assumption, therefore, is that competency in grammar and agility with sentence forms can improve students' writing ability as well as their chances for success beyond college. Simply put, students can use grammar to become better writers and better thinkers. So while this workbook does not make a *sine qua non* argument about curriculum that must be included in writing courses, it could not have been produced were it not for the fact that so many high school and college students do not learn certain core concepts of grammar, style, and structure.

So many families and educators rightfully reject the Common Core and other rule-from-abroad initiatives that have been rammed down the throats of teachers and students. A better approach would have been a bottom-up local conversation about what students should learn, when, and why they need to learn it; but teachers, because of their allergy to "should," have resisted engaging in such conversations for too long. Very often, when someone tells us what we *should* do, we feel rankled by this threat to our liberty and independence of mind. Some people, especially those in academia, bristle at the idea of "should," particularly when the obligation is externally imposed. Nevertheless, discussions about what students ought to learn serve teachers and educational institutions by promoting crucial discussions about goals and purpose and by encouraging members of institutions to get together in a spirited exchange of opposing viewpoints about what students should learn. Discussions about outcomes provide teachers with opportunities to learn about each other's pedagogical values and foster communication between and among teachers at all levels, which is crucial for achieving the ultimate goal of education: serving students.

We should have a national conversation about outcomes, but it should occur first at the local level (within communities, across departments and campuses). That conversation should address what students should learn, when they should learn it, and why they need to learn it. There are some useful models we can revisit for such undertakings. In 1939, John. C. Hodges, who wrote the *Harbrace College Handbook*, initiated a massive grassroots undertaking designed to find out what types of errors teachers note on student writing. He gathered twenty thousand sample of student papers that had been commented upon by instructors and evaluated the comments to create a "taxonomy of errors," which became the organizational structure of his influential textbook.[1] Decades later, Andrea Lunsford and Robert Connors, who wrote *The St. Martin's Handbook,* another very influential grammar and writing manual, conducted a similar study of patterns of error and patterns of instructor commentary (aspects instructors chose to comment on and aspects instructors chose not to comment on). The work of researchers like Hodges, Lunsford, and Connors is important because it shows us a way to build a dialogue about the principles of composition that institutions value. Their work, however, presents only part of the conversation and part of the process that *should* occur at every educational institution. We should not merely ask, as many books do, what errors do teachers notice? We should also ask, what errors *should* teachers notice? What errors will readers notice when students write outside of the classroom? What can be done to change or reinforce perceptions about the relative and comparative importance of certain types of writing deficiencies (grammatical, substantive, stylistic, etc.)? Writing instructors like to teach students about audience, but how often do they consider that students will not always be writing for an audience that shares the composition values that their instructors, institutions, and communities have? If we have a conversation that includes all members of the constituencies we serve (students, parents, the workforce, exam makers, et al), we will better serve our students.

This book was produced in response to the gaps in writing competency between and among students I teach. My experiences as a student and a teacher, and the examples of my students demonstrate that the lack of conversation about outcomes has been a disservice to students, whose knowledge bases are affected by the lack of continuity in instruction at all levels. Furthermore, this lack of consensus about composition objectives places a huge burden on students who are poor and affords great advantages to the wealthy. Wealthy students can pay tutors to prepare them for the content on standardized exams. They can hire experts to ensure that their writing meets the standards of the best colleges; they can pay for help with resume writing so that they can earn the best jobs, and they can, in general, pay to eliminate every gap in their education. I myself am a private tutor, paid to help economically advantaged students when their teachers aren't preparing them for exams and writing assignments, when their guidance counselors aren't providing the assistance they need with college applications, and when their education hasn't prepared them for the writing demands of college composition courses.

This lack of a grassroots conversation has led to some very dubious top-down edicts from educational central planners who do not know how to address the individual needs of students at the local level. Because we haven't had these conversations, teachers are losing academic freedom to educational central planners, parents are losing their influence and knowledge of local curricula, and students' reading and writing abilities have plateaued. What a painful irony that our quixotic fight for freedom from *should* has afforded corporate lobbyists and out-of-touch academic and political elites the opportunity to *mandate* what we *must* teach, when, and how. As a consequence, we will all (students, parents, and teachers, administrators) chafe under a far more oppressive and educationally foolish system.

While working within this system, we can work to transform it from within by producing books, like this, that address the needs of the students we teach. There are many useful composition books, but finding *one* that meets the needs of most students is very difficult. Some composition books are too dense, discouraging students and professors from accessing their information. Others are too expensive, posing obstacles to access to resources that many of us, especially at community colleges, find unpalatable. Still others are just right in size and price, but their scope is distorted, failing to offer the content that students need. Having been frustrated by this Goldilocks textbook odyssey, I wanted a single book that I could use to teach writing. I wrote this book, hoping it would strike just the right balance by introducing core concepts in grammar and style and providing practice with those concepts.

Drawing on my experiences as a high school English teacher, a professor of composition and literature at Suffolk County Community College, a private tutor and college advisor, and a writing center coordinator, this book offers what I hope to be the porridge students need in order to improve on the fundamental aspects of writing. That porridge has two main ingredients: references and exercises. More workbook than reference guide, *Deconstructing and Reconstructing Sentences* is designed to provide practice with fundamental concepts in composition, but especially concepts in grammar and style. When a theory or concept is discussed, such as what a verb is and how it functions, I have employed a minimalist approach, assuming that whatever students can't grasp, instructors will clarify. Like athletes and any other competent professionals, writers learn by *doing* and *reflecting* on what they do, so most of the material here is practical and product-based, rather than theoretical and reading-based. Since the book has a reference component in every chapter, it should serve users as a useful reference guide beyond its service to a particular course.

Since there seems to be a movement nationally (and in my state of New York) to shift to a core knowledge approach to curriculum, especially in the languages, and since this movement is already reflected in the grammar and writing portions of standardized exams such as the SAT and ACT, students at the primary and secondary levels will benefit from the content of this book.

That content, selected with the assumption that there are certain core principles of composition writers must understand, includes the following:

- Practice identifying and applying major parts of sentences, such as verbs, adverbs, adjectives and nouns, relative clauses, conjunctions, and several other foundational sentence elements.
- Exercises in major concepts in grammar, such as fragments and run-ons, agreement errors, and punctuation.
- Activities that provide practice with elements of sentence and paragraph anatomy and physiology, including paragraph unity, topic sentence function, transitions, and sentence combining.
- Opportunities for students to experiment with techniques for achieving creative titles, writing effective openings/introductions and closings/conclusions, and many chances to build sentence variety.

- Concise references to technical and stylistic matters, such as using parenthetical citations, incorporating quotes, and explaining the function of a works cited page.

Organized so that instructors can select topics *a la carte* or provide enrichment tailored to the individual needs of students, the book affords users flexibility and accessibility. Each topic, introduced by a brief discussion of the content (the theorizing) and followed by exercises that provide practice applying that content (the doing), is presented with the goal of teaching students how to incorporate the ideas into their writing. The goal is to provide a minimal amount of theorizing and a maximum amount of opportunities for students to experiment with and apply the ideas they encounter. Ultimately, the book *should* introduce students to a variety of techniques for forming a clean sentence in English and for becoming independent writers and critical readers with a broad composition knowledge base.

—Joe Gansrow

Part I

PARTS OF SENTENCES
AND THEIR FUNCTIONS

Topics Covered

1. Subjects and Verbs
2. Prepositions and Prepositional Phrases
3. Nouns
4. Pronouns
5. Adjectives and Adverbs
6. Clauses
7. Conjunctions

INTRODUCTION TO PARTS OF SENTENCES AND THEIR FUNCTIONS

A sentence can be a question:
How are you?

Or a statement:
I am well.

It can be an exclamation:
Let there be light!

Sentences can be *simple* in form or meaning, with only one subject and verb:
Dogs growl at strangers.

And, much to our dismay, sentences can be complex in form or meaning, with multiple subjects and verbs:
My friend, who doesn't always tell the truth, will remain my friend because she forgives me for my transgressions.

Did You Know?

Sentences can be as short as a *single word*. The first line of Charles Dickens's *Bleak House* is only one word long: "London." Want to try a long sentence? Read the final sentence of James Joyce's *Ulysses* if you dare: it's almost thirteen thousand words long!

Some even define sentences as the space between two marks of terminal punctuation (all the words between periods, period and exclamation point, question mark and period, etc.).

Just because a sentence is simple or short doesn't mean it can't express a complex idea. In fact, many believe that it takes much more effort and skill to craft an effective *short* sentence than it takes to compose an effective long sentence.

The conventional way that grammarians define a sentence is as a group of words containing a subject (whom or what the sentence is about) and a predicate (information about the subject, including the verb). For our purposes, let's think along the lines of the conventional grammarians, classifying groups of words as sentence when they express complete thoughts and contain subjects and verbs.

A Few Reasons to Learn Parts of Sentences

This section provides techniques for identifying important parts of sentences and practice learning the functions of those essential sentence elements. Knowing how sentence parts functions is as crucial for writers as it is for doctors to know how body parts function. Do you think that for doctors the word "lung" or how a lung functions can be good at their trade? Why should it be different for writers and writing? In the pages that follow, you'll learn how to identify parts of sentences (sentence anatomy) and their functions (sentence physiology), which will help you with your writing, thinking, and reading comprehension.

1

SUBJECTS AND VERBS

Almost every sentence has a subject and verb. The **most important** part of a sentence and probably the *most important* part of speech is the **verb**.

Whether you're trying to write an effective sentence or interpret one, think first about verbs. Whenever possible, resist the temptation to rely on the verb *to be* (see below) in your writing because it tends *to be* imprecise.

Verbs

Verbs are about *action* or *being*.

Examples of **action verbs**: smash, talk, eat, mumble, groan, steal, ask

Shakespeare **wrote** many plays. [*wrote*=an action]

Examples of the **verb to be**: am, is, are, was, were, has been, have been, had been

My father **was** an affectionate man. [*was*=a being verb]

Verbs in Disguise

In football, normally the quarterback receives the snap and then either hands off or passes. Sometimes, however, the quarterback chooses to run the ball himself or even to block or receive a pass. He's still the quarterback, but in those other cases, he's functioning like a running back, blocker, or receiver. Verbs are versatile, like quarterbacks. Verbs function in various ways, acting as **nouns** and **adjectives**, and sometimes as the **subject** of a sentence. When you read and write, ask whether these disguised verbs describe nouns (in which case they're acting as adjectives) or if they're pretending to be nouns themselves. See the examples below, which feature chameleon-like verbs.

> **Reading Tip**
>
> If you're having trouble interpreting a sentence, find verbs first. If you find the verb, you can more easily find the subject. If you identify subject and verb, you have the main idea of a sentence.

Example: I parked the car. [*parked* functions as a conventional **verb**, providing the action]

Example: Parking is difficult. *parking* functions as a **noun** and the subject of the verb *is*]

Example: The driver crashed into a parked car. [*parked* functions as an **adjective**, modifying the noun *car*]

Exercise 1.1a Identifying Verbs

1. Which list contains **verbs** only? Circle the letter that corresponds to your choice.

   (a) sip, stab, is, are, am, had, grumble, grab
   (b) sip, stab, is, was, golden, car, bold, filthy

2. Identify at least one word that is *NOT* a verb in 1a or 1b. _____

3. Which list contains **verbs** only? Circle the letter that corresponds to your choice.

   (a) crawl, step, were, weigh, feel, need, look, throw
   (b) am, normally, steer, yesterday, want, ferocious, old, orange

4. Identify at least one word that is *NOT* a verb in 3a or 3b. _____

5. Which list contains **verbs** only? Circle the letter that corresponds to your choice.

   (a) under, near, by, with, for, to, bathe, women
   (b) go, take, reject, accept, understand, ignore

6. Identify at least one word that is *not* a verb in 5a or 5b.

   _____

7. Which list contains **verbs** only? Circle the letter that corresponds to your choice.

   (a) gargle, rinse, spit, spray, gush, cleanse
   (b) slowly, carefully, defiantly, definitely

8. Identify at least one word that is *not* a verb in 7a or 7b.

   _____

9. Add at least two writing-related verbs to the following list, and feel free to consult a <u>thesaurus</u> if you'd like: scribble, write, _____

   _____

10. Add at least two speaking-related verbs to the following list, and feel free to consult a <u>thesaurus</u> if you'd like: say, relate, _____

Subjects

Every sentence has a **subject**, which is **what the sentence is about**. But it's often not useful to define the subject as what the sentence is about since sentences can have many subjects. It's helpful to think of the subject as who or what is acting on the verb.

Without a subject, a sentence is usually incomplete—**a fragment** and it's likely going to be unclear.

A sentence's subject can be a person, place, thing, action, verb, noun—almost anything you can think of. Since the subject of a sentence is often a person, place, or thing, and since we know that people, places, and things are classified as **nouns**, we tend to think, mistakenly, that any noun we find is the subject. Not every noun is the subject.

As discussed above, the subject is what the sentence is about—the main idea—but in grammatical terms, the <u>subject</u> is **who/what acts on the verb**. If you can find the verb, you can find the subject. If you know the subject and verb, you understand the core of the sentence, which is crucial for reading comprehension and analyzing your writing. The grammatical subject and verb are the main idea of a sentence.

> *** Trouble Spot**
>
> Some parts of speech, such as prepositional phrases, seem like subjects, but they aren't. Some students confuse prepositional phrases with subjects. See sections 2.2 and 2.3 to learn how to avoid such sinister traps.

How to Find the Subject

(1) First find the verb. (2) Ask *Who/what is acting on the verb? Who/what is "verbing"?* (3) Then place subject and verb next to each other to see if they make sense.

Example: Shakespeare **wrote** many plays.

1. *wrote*=a verb 2. who/what wrote? *Shakespeare* 3. *Shakespeare*=the subject

> *** Reminder**
> Sentences can have more than one subject and verb.

Exercise 1.1b   Subjects and Verbs in Context

<u>Directions</u>: Circle the best answer.

1. Group work is more enjoyable than individual work.

    A. *work* is the verb; *group* is the subject of *work*
    B. *is* is the verb; *individual* is the subject of *is*
    C. *is* is the verb; *group work* is the subject of *is*

2. When I work in groups, I talk incessantly.

    A. *incessantly* is the verb; *groups* is the subject of *incessantly*
    B. *work* is the verb; *talk* is the subject of *work*
    C. *work and talk* are the verbs; *I* is the subject of *work* and *talk*

3. My untrained dog piddles in the house and barks loudly, but my friend's poodle is house trained and never barks.

    A. *untrained* is the verb; *dog* and *poodle* are the subjects of *never*
    B. *dog* is the subject of the verbs *piddles* and *barks; poodle* is the subject of the verbs *is* and *barks*
    C. *house, poodle* and *dog* are subjects; *untrained* and *loudly* are verbs

4. Although I usually don't eat sweets, tonight I gorged on chocolate bars, brownies, and butterscotch pudding.

    A. *I* is the subject of the verbs *eat* and *gorged*
    B. *Chocolate bars, brownies,* and *butterscotch pudding* are the subjects; *sweets* is the verb

C. There is only one verb in this sentence: *eat*

5. During the summer, Irfan and Marcha traveled to Trinidad, but Julie and Stashanna stayed at home.

   A. *summer* is the subject; *traveled* is the verb
   B. *Irfan* and *Marcha* are the subjects of the verb *traveled; Julie* and *Stashana* are the subjects of the verb *stayed*
   C. *traveled* and *stayed* are verbs; *Trinidad* is the subject

6. Eating smoked sausage makes me ill.

   A. *ill* is the subject; *smoking* is the verb
   B. *ill* is the subject; *makes* is the verb
   C. *Eating* is a verb acting as a noun and the subject of the verb *makes*; s*moked* is also a verb, and it's acting as an adjective describing the noun *sausage*

7. Studying the night before an exam is crucial for success.

   A. *before* is the verb; *night* is the subject
   B. *Studying* is the verb; *night* is the subject
   C. *Studying* is a verb acting as a noun and as the subject of the verb *is*

8. Do you see the poor man on the corner?

   A. *you* is the subject; *see* is the verb
   B. *man* is the subject; *do* is the verb
   C. *corner* is the subject; *see* is the verb

9. Using a thesaurus will help you with vocabulary and precision.

   A. *you* is the subject of the verb *will help*
   B. *Using* is a verb functioning as a noun and as the subject of the verb *will help*
   C. *thesaurus* and *you* are subjects; *precision* and *help* are verbs

10. My favorite part of speech is the verb; my mother's favorite part of speech is the adjective.

   A. *My* and *speech* are subjects; *verb* and *part* are verbs
   B. *part* and *verb* are subjects; *speech* is a verb
   C. *part* is the subject; *is* is a verb

* Trouble Spot

A sentence's main idea, which is the main subject and verb, is usually in the main/independent clause, not in the dependent/subordinate clause. For more on clauses see section 1.6.

Exercise 1.1c
More Subjects and Verbs

<u>Directions</u>: In the space below each sentence, identify subjects and verbs. There might be more than one subject and verb in each sentence.

Example: I snuggle with my puppy.
Verb: <u>snuggle</u>   Subject: <u>I</u>

1. I drove my car too fast.

Verb(s):_____Subject(s):_____

2. She is pretty.

Verb(s):_____Subject(s):_____

3. Spencer studies every night, even when he is exhausted.

Verb(s):_____Subject(s):_____

4. Arguing in front of children causes them a great deal of pain.

Verb(s):_____Subject(s):_____

5. After I chugged three glasses of water, I belched loudly, which angered my wife.

Verb(s):_____Subject(s):_____

6. She laughed, cried, and then screamed when she heard the miraculous news.

Verb(s):_____Subject(s):_____

7. I knew him for only one year, but the professor was a friend and a mentor.

Verb(s):_____Subject(s):_____

> *** Trouble Spot**
>
> In most sentences, the subject comes *before* the verb. However, some sentences, especially those with prepositional phrases and sentences that begin with "here" or "there" might violate the rule about the subject preceding verb.

8. Nothing smells better than percolating coffee in the morning.

Verb(s): _____ Subject(s): _____

9. There is a softshell turtle at the bottom of the pond.

Verb(s):_____Subject(s):_____

10. All this time Sancho was on the hill, watching his master's follies, tearing his beard and cursing. [*Don Quixote*]

Verb(s):_____Subject(s):_____

*Write a sentence that *begins with a verb*. Identify the subject(s) and verb(s).

_____

_____

_____

_____

_____

_____

Verb(s):_____Subject(s):_____

2

PREPOSITIONS

Prepositions usually appear *before* a noun or pronoun, establishing a relationship between nouns, pronouns, and other parts of the sentence. Often short words that indicate direction or location, prepositions must be memorized in order to be recognized. One of many very annoying and inconsistent aspects of grammar is that we classify some concepts by function (verbs, for example, indicate action/being), but we do not classify others, such as articles (a, an, the) and prepositions that way.

Some very **common prepositions**: *at, by, from, in, of, on, to*, and *with*.

More Prepositions: about, above, across, after, against, ahead of, along, alongside, amid, among, before, behind, below, beneath, beside, between, despite, during, following, for, inside, near, next, off, onto, out, outside, over, past, through, throughout, toward, under, until, up, upon, within, without

A **PREPOSITIONAL PHRASE** is comprised of a <u>preposition</u> and its <u>object</u>. The object of a preposition is a <u>noun</u> or a <u>pronoun</u>.

Preposition (in) + Object (the water) =
Prepositional Phrase (in the water)

Note that a prepositional phrase can contain articles or adjectives.

Example: for the old lady. For = preposition, the = article, old = adjective, and lady = noun

Since the object of a preposition is a <u>noun</u> or a <u>pronoun</u>, writers occasionally confuse the object of the preposition with the subject of a sentence. **The subject of a sentence is never in the prepositional phrase**.

Be aware that sentences can have back-to-back prepositional phrases.

Example: You'll find the keys <u>in the kitchen</u> <u>on the counter</u> <u>near the refrigerator</u>.

The preposition *to* + verb is *not* a prepositional phrase. This construction is merely the infinitive form of the verb.

- to eat
- to drink

If you want to improve on **reading comprehension**, add **variety** to your sentences, and reduce the chance that you'll make a subject-verb agreement error, make sure you can identify prepositional phrases. It's a good idea to *begin some sentences with prepositional phrases* in order to emphasize key ideas and create **sentence variety**.

Exercise 1.2a Identifying Prepositions

1. Which list contains **prepositions** only? Circle the letter that corresponds to your choice.

    (a) with, for, by, near, under, to, toss, slowly, uncle
    (b) at, before, of, until, over, past, throughout, during

2. Identify at least one word that is *NOT* a preposition in a or b. _____

3. Which list contains **prepositions** only? Circle the letter that corresponds to your choice.

    (a) ahead, during, off, prior, upon, through, along, toward, at
    (b) across, like, press, inside, down, against, solemn, potato, door

    Use Your Resources:

    Consult the list of prepositions at the beginning of this section, and the theories about them, in order to answer the questions in the preposition exercises.

4. Identify at least one word that is *not* a preposition in a or b. _____

5. Using the preposition table at the beginning of this section and your knowledge of parts of sentences (nouns, verbs, adjectives, etc.), create a list of five words like those in questions one and three. Some of the words should be prepositions, but some shouldn't.

    A. _____
    B. _____
    C. _____
    D. _____

E. _____

F. Identify at least one word from 5 A-E that is *not* a preposition. _____

6. Is a prepositional phrase ever going to contain the subject of a sentence? _____

7. A prepositional phrase has two main parts:
   _____ and _____

8. The object of a preposition is usually a _____ or a _____

9. In the space provided, write the words that are NOT part of the prepositional phrases.

   A. snow on the ground

   _____

   B. soaring high above the earth

   _____

   C. drove with Owen and Anna

   _____

   D. played near the pear tree

   _____

10. Write a sentence that begins with a prepositional phrase.

_____

_____

_____

_____

Exercise 1.2b Distinguishing Prepositional Phrases, Subjects, and Verbs

Directions: ~~Strike through~~ the prepositional phrases in the following sentences. Then identify the subjects and verbs in the space below each sentence.

1. A large portion of the proceeds will be allocated for food and clothing.

Verb(s):_____Subject(s):_____

2. On Saturday, I'm going to the mall with Rick and John to buy microphones for the concert.

Verb(s):_____Subject(s):_____

3. The stains on the lampshade were produced by a cigarette that you left in the ashtray.

Verb(s):_____Subject(s):_____

4. Out of the cradle, endlessly rocking, from your sad memories, dear brother, I sing reminiscence. [Paraphrased
5. from a Walt Whitman poem.]

Verb(s):_____Subject(s)._____

6. In the kitchen, on the counter near the microwave, you'll find the keys alongside the cookie jar.

Verb(s):_____Subject(s):_____

7. In the summer, I drink lemonade and eat strawberries.

Verb(s):_____Subject(s):_____

8. My brother, along with two of his annoying friends, went with me to the mall on Friday to buy Nikes.

Verb(s):_____Subject(s):_____

9. Across the street from my house lives Boo Radley, a reclusive fellow.

Verb(s):_____Subject(s):_____

10. Upon the brimming water among the stones are nine and fifty swans. [Paraphrased from a Yeats poem.)

Verb(s):_____Subject(s):_____

11. The brutal nurse stuck the needle into the wrong vein, so blood flowed from my arm while she again jabbed the needle beneath my skin.

Verb(s): _____
Subject(s): _____

Remember

Sometimes an *adjective* will precede the noun or pronoun in the prepositional phrase as in the following example: *with my broken hand.* The prepositional phrase includes all words between the preposition and the noun/pronoun that comes at the end of the prepositional phrase. For more on adjectives, see section 1.5.

Exercise 1.2c Identifying Subjects, Verbs, and Prepositions

<u>Directions:</u> Circle the letter that corresponds to the best answer.

1. Near my house you'll find a waste management facility. You'll smell it too.

   A. The sentence begins with a prepositional phrase
   B. *my house* is the subject of the sentence

2. Blowing in the wind is the answer.

   A. *the wind* is the object of the preposition
   B. The sentence begins with a form of the verb to be

3. He was living just enough for the city. [Taken from a Stevie Wonder song.]

   A. *for the city* is a prepositional phrase
   B. *He* is a verb

4. Are you a lucky little lady in the city of light, or just another lost angel? [Taken from a Doors song.]

   A. The sentence begins with a form of the verb to be
   B. The sentence does NOT have back-to-back prepositional phrases

5. I am the king of rock—there is none higher. [Taken from a Run DMC song.]

   A. The subject of the sentence is *rock*

B. *rock* is part of the prepositional phrase, so it can't be the subject

6. Out here in the fields, I fight for my meals. [Taken from a Who song.]

   A. *fields* and *meals* are subjects
   B. *fields* and *meals* are objects of prepositions, so they can't be subjects

7. Your plans have come to naught, and your life is half a page of scribbled lines. [Taken from a Pink Floyd song.]

   A. The sentence ends with a prepositional phrase
   B. *scribbled lines* is the subject of the sentence

8. The mass of people lead lives of quiet desperation. [Taken from Thoreau.]

   A. *people* is the subject of the sentence
   B. *lead* is a verb

9. I get by with a little help from my friends. [Taken from a Beatles song.]

   A. *I* is the subject of the sentence
   B. *my friends* is the subject of the sentence

10. After skiing, my girlfriend and I sip hot chocolate near the fire.

    A. *fire* is the subject of the sentence
    B. *my girlfriend* and *I* are the subjects of the sentence

3

NOUNS

Identifying Nouns

Nouns identify **people**, **places**, **things**, and **ideas**. Look at some of the examples
below:

> People: Rick, sister, captain, daughter
> Places: Baton Rouge, Brentwood, ocean, heaven
> Things: lizard, salamander, stapler, door, toe, ball
> Ideas: love, anger, fear, distress, pain

There are several types of nouns, but the ones we're going to focus on are **concrete**, **abstract**, **proper**, and **verbal** nouns. Verbals, also known as **gerunds**, are verbs that act like nouns. Consider the following example:

> Driving is fun.
> [*Driving* is a verb that acts as a noun.]

Don't confuse nouns with subjects. Not every noun is a subject.

* Glance Back

For more on subjects, see section 1.1.

Example: My brother eats chicken and drinks Coke at Jones Beach.

In this sentence, the **nouns** include *brother*, *chicken*, *Coke*, and *Jones Beach* since they all are people, places, or things. The **subject**, however, is *my brother*. We know this because the subject is the part of a sentence that acts on the verb (who/what loves to eat and to drink?).

Look at the table below for ways to identify nouns:

Type of Noun	Concrete	Abstract	Proper	Verbal
Characteristics	Think five senses: these nouns can be seen, heard, felt, tasted, and/ or touched.	Can't be detected by the five senses.	Identify particular people, places, and things. Must be capitalized.	Look like verbs because they end in –*ing*, but act like nouns.
Examples (noun type in bold)	**Dogs** drink **water** from **toilets**.	The dog's **curiosity** about toilet water intrigued me.	My dog **Pepper** drinks water from the toilet.	**Drinking** toilet water is disgusting.

Exercise 1.3a Identifying Nouns

1. Which list contains **nouns** only? Circle the letter that corresponds to your choice.

    (a) dog, decide, computer, roof, tree, with, admit, cloudy

(b) cat, decision, desk, nail, leaf, song, admission, cloud

2. Identify at least one word that is *not* a noun in a or b.

   _____

3. Which list contains **nouns** only? Circle the letter that corresponds to your choice.

   (a) was, examine, near, pencil, from, Rivera, commitment, injure
   (b) book, flower, missile, professor, scallop, message, building, injury

4. Identify at least one word that is *not* a noun in a or b.

   _____

5. Use the thesaurus to add at least two college-related nouns to the following list: <u>professor, whiteboard,</u>

   _____

Exercise 1.3b Classifying Nouns

<u>Directions:</u> Use the word bank to find the noun type that best classifies the way the italicized nouns function.

Concrete	Abstract	Proper	Verbal

1. *Digging* holes is grueling work. _   _____

2. Indiana Jones, equipped with *lasso* and *revolver*, searches for *treasure* and battles the Nazis. _____

3. *Neo* is played by *Keanu Reeves* in the movie *The Matrix*, and *Reeves* also plays quarterback *Shane Falco* in *The Replacements*. _____

4. The audience jeered at Hartnett's *performance* of "Gunga Din." _____

5. I gorge on *fries, hot dogs, soda,* and *snowcaps* while at the *theatre*. _____

6. *Screws, nails, shims, saws, hammers, caulk, sawdust,* vibrations, frustration, *sweat, stink,* and labor contributed to the framing of the *set* of the movie. _____

7. *Watching* movies and *eating* popcorn are enjoyable. _____

8. He said *Professor Jones* is a great professor, but I think that he is one of the more incompetent professors at *Marshall College*. _____

9. I cringe when Russell Crowe talks about his *anger* and *frustration*, or when any actor lectures me about *politics*. _____

10. *Freedom, tradition, love,* and *sacrifice* distinguish the great films, thematically, from the films I don't rate as highly. _____

Exercise 1.3c Identifying Nouns in Context

<u>Directions</u>: In the space below each sentence, identify the nouns. There might be more than one noun in each sentence.

> * Note
>
> *Pronouns* (I, you, he/she/it, they, me, your, etc.) are not nouns. For more on pronouns see Section 1.4.

1. Rivera saved the game for the Yankees.
   Nouns: _____

2. Don't drink sour milk.
   Nouns: _____

3. Puffy clouds interest me more than blue skies.
   Nouns: _____

4. My roof leaks, so I hired a man to repair it.
   Nouns: _____

5. Greedy children will not receive presents from Santa.
   Nouns: _____

6. Slimy frogs and reclusive toads are my favorite amphibians.
   Nouns: _____

7. Sunglasses block ultraviolet rays.
   Nouns: _____

8. Ice cream and cookies taste better than cake and pudding.
   Nouns: _____

9. The old man is frail.

    Nouns: _____

10. Gulliver urinated on the fire.

    Nouns: _____

A. Write a sentence that begins with a verbal noun.

_____

_____

_____

_____

_____

_____

B. Write a sentence that begins with a list of at least three concrete nouns.

_____

_____

_____

_____

_____

_____

4

PRONOUNS

Pronouns serve as substitutes for nouns.

Example: Rick drove to the mall to buy a shirt, but he forgot his wallet.

Dissection: Here, the pronoun *he* substitutes for the noun "Rick."

Without pronouns, sentences would be very awkward and repetitive. Consider this **Example:** Rick drove to the mall to buy a shirt, but Rick forgot Rick's wallet.

Unfortunately, as you'll see later in this chapter and in sections 2.4–2.7, pronouns can create quite a bit of mischief, especially agreement errors and lack of clarity when we try to write or interpret a sentence, so it's important to master pronouns.

There are several types of pronouns. We're going to focus on four: **Subject**, **Object**, **Possessive**, and **Reflexive**. See the table below for examples.

PERSON	SUBJECT Identify subject/make sense next to verb	OBJECT Receive action of verb	POSSESSIVE Show ownership or possession	REFLEXIVE Refer to subject of sentence/a prior pronoun
first person	I	me	my, mine	myself
second person	you	you	your, yours	yourself
third person	he, she, it	him, her, it	his, her, hers, its	himself, herself, itself
first person plural	we	us	our, ours	ourselves
second person plural	you	you	your, yours	yourselves
third person plural	they	them	their, theirs	themselves

* Demonstrative Pronouns

One type of pronoun not mentioned in the chart is the demonstrative pronoun, which includes the following: *this, that, these,* and *those.*

Exercise 1.4a   Identifying Pronouns

1. Which list contains **pronouns** only? Circle the letter that corresponds to your choice.

   (a) I, they, your, myself, their, his, us, you
   (b) I, they, with, under, their, for, from, belch

2. Identify at least one word that is *NOT* a pronoun in a or b. _____

3. Which list contains **possessive** pronouns only?

   (a) my, your, their, our, his, her, its
   (b) my, you, it, you, we, himself, she

4. Which list contains **object** pronouns only?

   (a) him, her, them, us,
   (b) ourselves, I, themselves

5. Which list contains **subject** pronouns only?

   (a) I, you, her, his, mine, yours
   (b) I, you, he, she, it, we, they

ANTECEDENTS

Pronouns usually have **antecedents**. An **antecedent** is the word or phrase that a pronoun refers to. In the following sentence, note that the antecedent of *his* is *Walter Kirby*. You can substitute *Walter Kirby* for *his* and vice versa.

Walter Kirby shared his gift with his friends.

When you write, make sure your **pronouns** clearly refer to their **antecedents**. Similarly, when you read, make sure you can link pronouns with their antecedents; otherwise, your comprehension will suffer.

Exercise 1.4b   Pronouns and Their Antecedents

<u>Directions</u>: Indicate the antecedent of the italicized pronoun in each of the following sentences.

1. Whenever my mother scolds me, I get a little frustrated with *her.* _____

2. If dad doesn't prepare mom's coffee with milk and sugar, she gets mad at *him.* _____

3. That dish on the countertop needs to be put away before *it* slides off and breaks. _____

4. Mike's phone rings anytime his friends want something from *him.* _____

5. The earth revolves around the sun, orbiting *it* once a year. _____

6. The judge, foolishly, does not base his decisions on precedent or rational arguments; instead, he grounds *them* in irrationality. _____

7. When she asked me if we completed the chores, I told her that I did them all, and did them *myself.*

    _____

8. There is something that doesn't love a wall—something that sends the frozen ground under *it*, causing the wall to dilapidate (taken from a Frost poem).

    _____

9. He said his prayers, *this* ancient holy man.

_____

10. Cannons to the left of *them*, cannons to the right of them, and cannons in front of them, yet into the jaws of death and into the mouth of hell rode the six hundred (taken from a Tennyson poem). _____

> * Did You Know?
>
> **Antecedent** is not, etymologically speaking, always a correct way to describe word order with pronouns. Antecedent implies referring to something before (ante), but in some cases, antecedents come *after* pronouns, acting more as *postcedents* than antecedents.

5

ADJECTIVES AND ADVERBS

Adjectives and adverbs are two of the more important parts of speech for improving the **descriptive** aspects of your writing and for creating **tone**. These parts of speech help writers with several goals, but especially the following:

- The creation of descriptive sentences
- Clarity of expression
- Development of tone and mood
- Persuasion

What is an adjective?

Adjectives modify (provide more information about and develop the meaning of) <u>nouns and pronouns</u>. Usually, they precede the words they modify.

Example: The professor yelled.

Dissection: This sentence has no adjective, no word describing the noun *professor*.

Example: The cranky professor yelled.

Dissection: This sentence has an adjective, *cranky*, which describes/modifies the noun, *professor*.

Adjectives often answer the following questions: Which? What kind? How many?

Example: Four yellow snakes slithered past the younger man.

Dissection: *Four* reveals <u>how many</u> snakes, *yellow* reveals <u>what kind</u> of snakes, and *younger* reveals <u>which</u> man we're discussing.

What is an Adverb?

Adverbs modify verbs, adjectives, and other adverbs. Very often, adverbs end in –ly. Adverbs often answer the following questions: *How? Where? When?*

Example: The man drove down the street.

This sentence has no adverb, or word modifying the verb *drove*.

Example: The very nice man slowly drove down the street.

> **Technique**
> If you want to improve your writing, especially in the area of **detail**, incorporate more adjectives and adverbs into your sentences.

This sentence has an adverb, *very*, which modifies the adjective *nice*, and an adverb *slowly*, which modifies the verb *drove*.

Example: Everywhere I looked yesterday, I saw turtles lazily basking on logs.

Everywhere is an adverb (<u>where</u> the person looked), *yesterday* is an adverb (<u>when</u> the person looked), and *lazily* is an adverb (describes <u>how</u> the turtles bask).

Time words, especially those that indicate frequency, are often adverbs. Remember key time adverbs such as *today,* *tomorrow, yesterday, always, usually, sometimes, never,* and *often.*

Not every adverb ends in –ly. Some of the more common adverbs that do *not* end in –ly: very, there, here, and well.

> **Value of a Dictionary**
>
> If you have any doubts about how words function, consult a dictionary. If you want to know if a word is an adjective, verb, adverb, noun, etc, use the dictionary. Remember that some words can perform multiple functions.

Exercise 1.5a Identifying Adjectives and Adverbs

1. Which list contains **adjectives** only? Circle the letter that corresponds to your choice.

   (a) mysterious, frosty, patiently, hamburger, under, carefully, throw
   (b) mysterious, frigid, obnoxious, surly, grouchy, barbaric, sluggish

2. Identify at least one word that is *not* an adjective in a or b. _____

3. Which list contains **adverbs** only? Circle the letter that corresponds to your choice.

(a) yesterday, somewhere, eagerly, perceptively, shrewdly, boldly, insightfully

(b) annually, earlier, eager, perception, soup, shrewd, ugly

4. Identify at least one word that is *not* an adverb in a or b. _____

5. Write a sentence that **begins with an adverb** and write a second sentence that **begins with an adjective**. You should use the **thesaurus** to find an adverb that has to do with speed/rapidity or its opposite and to find an adjective that has to do with intelligence or its opposite.

Example: Foolishly ignoring my professor's offer of extra help, I earned a D on the essay. [*Foolishly* is the adverb of intelligence/its opposite.]

5A. Write a sentence that begins with an *adverb of speed*.

_____

_____

_____

_____

_____

5B. Write a sentence that begins with an *adjective of intelligence*.

_____

_____

_____

_____

_____

Exercise 1.5b   Adjectives and Adverbs in Context

<u>Directions 1–2</u>: Write *T* for true and *F* for false.

_____1. Adjectives modify or provide more information about nouns.

_____2. Adverbs modify or provide more information about pronouns and verbs.

<u>Directions 3–10</u>: Select the letter that corresponds to the best answer.

3. My old sneakers are much more comfortable than my new Reeboks.

    A. "old" is an adjective that modifies the noun "sneakers"
    B. "old" is an adverb that modifies the noun "sneakers"

4. With their sharp teeth, vicious wolves tore the poor deer to pieces.

    A. "sharp" and "vicious" are adverbs that modify the pronoun "their"
    B. "sharp" and "vicious" are adjectives that modify the nouns "teeth" and "wolves," respectively

5. Neatly print your name and address on the application.

    A. "Neatly" is an adjective that modifies the noun "name"

    B. "Neatly" is an adverb that modifies the verb "print"

6. Frequently, I submit my compositions even though I haven't carefully revised.

    A. "Frequently" and "carefully" are adverbs that modify the verbs "submit" and "revised" respectively

    B. "Frequently" and "carefully" are adjectives that modify the pronoun "I"

7. The rain pattered dismally against the window when I beheld the dull yellow eye of the creature (this question's language is adapted from Mary Shelley).

    A. "dismally" is an adverb that modifies the verb "pattered"

    B. "yellow" is an adverb that modifies the noun "rain"

8. The very kind man donated his kidney to save my life.

    A. "very" is an adjective that modifies the noun "kidney"

    B. "very" is an adverb that modifies the adjective "kind"

9. Six hundred men rode into the jaws of death (this question's language adapted from Tennyson).

    A. "Six hundred" is an adjective that modifies the noun "men"

    B. "Six hundred" is an adjective that modifies the noun "jaws"

10. Foolishly believing the words of the dishonest girl, the boy once again had his heart ripped out.

A. "dishonest" is an adverb that modifies the noun "girl"
B. "foolishly" is an adverb that modifies the verb "believing"

Exercise 1.5c   More Adjectives and Adverbs

Directions 1–5: **Circle** adjectives and underline adverbs in the following sentences. Note that some sentences might not have both adjectives and adverbs. Some have only *one* of those two parts of speech.

1. Odysseus arrogantly taunts the vengeful Polyphemus.

2. Unrelenting Poseidon prevents Odysseus from sailing home.

3. Faithful Telemachus seeks information about his father.

4. Calypso jealously guards Odysseus and does not want him to return to Ithaca.

5. Eventually, the resourceful Odysseus returns home and courageously defends his family.

Directions 6–10: Provide the information requested about each sentence.

6. Ambitious Claudius poisons his brother, King Hamlet.

A. Is "Ambitious" an adjective or adverb?

_____

B. What word does "Ambitious" modify?

_____

7. Devastated by the death of his father and by his mother's hasty marriage with Claudius, Hamlet is depressed and occasionally contemplates suicide. The Ghost of King Hamlet persistently haunts Prince Hamlet, urging him to avenge his father's murder.

A. Are "occasionally" and "persistently" adjectives or adverbs? _____
B. What words do the words in 7A modify?
_____and_____

8. Skeptical about the ghost's motives, clever Hamlet devises a plan to see if his uncle Claudius did in fact murder his father.

A. Is "clever" an adjective or adverb?

_____

B. What word does it modify?

_____

9. Hamlet rashly stabs the wrong man, mistakenly believing him to be Claudius, the murderer of his father.

A. Is "rashly" an adjective or adverb?

_____

B. What word does it modify?

_____

10. At the end of the play, Hamlet avenges his father by killing Claudius, but devious Claudius poisons Hamlet.

A. Is "devious" an adjective or adverb?

_____

B. What word does *devious* modify?

_____

* Write a sentence that begins with an **adverb**.

_____

_____

_____

_____

_____

* Write a sentence that begins with an **adjective**.

_____

_____

_____

_____

_____

6

CLAUSES

A sentence is comprised of **clauses**. A <u>clause</u> is a group of words that contains a subject and a verb.

Examples:

1. since you study (you=subject, study=verb)
2. you do well on exams (you=subject, do=verb)

   A sentence can have more than one clause, but it *must* have at least one **independent clause.**
   An <u>independent clause</u> is a full sentence. If you read it, you would consider it a complete sentence because it can stand on its own.

Examples:

1. you will excel in this class
2. he believes in me

A **subordinate**, or **dependent clause,** is *not* a complete sentence. It's a fragment without an independent clause to rely on.

Examples:

1. if you devote time to revision
2. while I was dreaming

Clauses create variety, complexity, and detail; they shift the emphasis and modify the meaning of ideas in other parts of the sentence.

Exercise 1.6a
Identifying Dependent and Independent Clauses

Directions (1–5): In the space next to the question, identify the **boldfaced words** as either independent clauses (IND) or dependent clauses (D).

_____1. **He saw her from the bottom of the stairs** before she saw him. [Adapted from Frost]
_____2. **While winter winds blow,** seeds lie like corpses within their graves. [Adapted from Shelley.]
_____3. With an eye made quiet by the power of harmony, **we see into the life of things.** [Adapted from Wordsworth]
_____4. Out of my weakness and my melancholy, **he abuses me to damn me.** [Adapted from Shakespeare]
_____5. **In order to possess what you do not possess,** you must go by the way of dispossession. [Adapted from Eliot]

Directions (6–10): Each of the following sentences has two clauses: one <u>underlined</u>, one **bold**. Identify each clause as independent or dependent by writing IND or DP above the corresponding part of the sentence.

6. <u>Whether I shall turn out to be the hero of my own life,</u> **these pages must show.** [adapted from Dickens]

7. **If you can trust yourself when all doubt you,** <u>the world will be yours.</u> [adapted from Kipling]

8. <u>Although it is unaware and unthinking,</u> **the crowd is cheering.** [adapted from Williams]

9. **The nineteenth autumn has come upon me** <u>since I first made my count.</u> [adapted from Yeats]

10. <u>This anxiety is common to all</u> **when they set their sights on anything so high.**

A. Write a sentence that has a dependent and an independent clause.

_____

_____

_____

_____

_____

7

CONJUNCTIONS

Conjunctions <u>connect</u> parts of a sentence.

Conjunctions perform several important functions, including the following:

- Establish relationships between and among ideas in a sentence.
- Clarify the meaning of sentences.
- Increase writers' options for conveying ideas.
- Afford chances for adding variety and style to sentences.

Two of the more important conjunction types are **coordinating** and **subordinating** conjunctions.

Coordinating conjunctions <u>join equal parts</u> of a sentence together.

An easy way to remember **coordinating conjunctions** is by the acronym **FANBOYS** (*for, and, nor, but, or, yet, so*). Coordinating conjunctions need a comma before FANBOYS when they join two independent clauses.

Subordinating conjunctions <u>connect the main clause to a dependent clause</u>. That is, subordinating conjunctions connect clauses that *can't* stand alone to clauses that *can* stand alone.

There are many **subordinating conjunctions**. Here is a list of some of the more common ones: after, although, as, because, before, even though, if, in order, now that, once, rather than, since, so that, that, than, though, unless, when, while, where, wherever

Exercise 1.7a   Conjunctions

<u>Directions</u>: Circle the letter that corresponds to the conjunction that best completes the sentence.

1. Larry Bird was slow, _____ he was good.

    A. and
    B. although
    C. but

2. _____ Michael Jordan won six NBA championships and five MVP awards, he failed in his attempt to become a professional baseball player.

    A. Since
    B. Because
    C. Although

3. In the 1961–1962 season, Wilt Chamberlain averaged more than fifty points per game, _____ in 1967–1968 he led the league in assists.

A. so
B. and
C. for

4. Magic Johnson may have the second most triple-doubles ever, _____ in 1961–1962, before the stat was recorded on a game-by-game basis, Oscar Robertson averaged a triple-double for the entire season.

A. and
B. or
C. but

5. _____ he was such a private and understated man, Kareem Abdul-Jabbar, who won six MVP awards and six NBA championships, does not receive the recognition that he deserves.

A. If
B. Though
C. Since

6. _____ many people remember him as a Senator from New Jersey, Bill Bradley had a successful NBA career, winning two NBA Championships with the Knicks and earning induction into the Hall of Fame in 1983.

A. While
B. Now that
C. For

7. Nicknamed "Mr. Clutch," Jerry West was one of the greatest players in basketball history, _____ he was also one of the greater executives in NBA history, serving

as General Manager during the Lakers' dynasty in the 1980s and drafting Kobe Bryant in 1996.

A. so
B. and
C. unless

8. In the 1983–1984 playoffs, Bernard King averaged almost forty points per game _____ he played with both of his middle fingers dislocated.

A. even though
B. because
C. or

9. Patrick Ewing never won an NBA championship, _____ he probably won't ever be considered as great as those centers, such as Russell, Chamberlain, Olajuwon, and O'Neal, who did win championships.

A. but
B. for
C. so

10. _____ played an additional season or two when their skills would have diminished, some of the great players retired when their talent was at or near its peak.

A. Because they
B. Rather than
C. While they

A. Write a sentence that begins with a subordinating conjunction.

_____

_____

_____

_____

_____

Part II

COMMON SENTENCE ERRORS

Topics Covered in this Part

1. Comma splices, run-ons, and fragments
2. Subject-verb agreement
3. Verb tense
4. Pronouns
5. Parallelism
6. Modifiers
7. Punctuation
8. Easily confused words

INTRODUCTION
TO COMMON SENTENCE
ERRORS

As you've probably observed during the course of your life, some people miss the big picture. This is true of your writing as well. You've written an insightful and compelling composition, but *those* people see only the comma splice or tense shift.

Some people, even professors, use their knowledge to establish their superiority over other people, hoping to elevate themselves by demeaning those who make a seemingly minor mistake. Highlighting your misuse of the fundamentals of grammar allows them to put you in your place. This intellectual bullying and carping is an objectionable trait, but not an uncommon one. Stand up to these pedantic bullies by carefully editing for grammar.

Similarly, and especially in a competitive job market, hiring committees need to find ways to distinguish job candidates, so they punish a resume, excessively, for a few blunders with key grammar concepts. Increase your job prospects by proofreading.

The priggishness of readers is not the only reason why writers should proofread carefully to ensure that their compositions avoid major grammatical errors. Grammatical errors obviously can affect clarity and comprehension, such as when a professor or employer has to pause to understand what the writer is presenting, or worse, has to waste time rereading and decoding ungrammatical sentences.

For all of these reasons and then some, it's important to learn how to identify major grammatical errors and eliminate them from your writing. Don't let your readers miss the big picture of your writing because you've made major grammatical errors. Don't let college admissions committees reject you because you didn't read your writing. Don't give employers a chance to eliminate you from consideration because you *didn't* revise carefully.

No study that I know of suggests that mastery of grammar is correlative with intelligence; however, erring with the major concepts can indicate to others that you haven't devoted enough time to your writing. That failure to devote time to your writing could suggest that you are someone who isn't thoughtful, determined, or prepared. That failure almost certainly will be interpreted as a major shortcoming.

Therefore, try to avoid making the errors you see in this unit.

8

RUN-ONS, COMMA SPLICES, AND FRAGMENTS

Three of the more common types of sentence errors are **comma splices**, **run-ons**, and **fragments**. As you revise, make sure that you join independent clauses correctly, and that you write in complete sentences.

Run-Ons

A run-on sentence occurs when two or more independent clauses are joined because of incorrect punctuation or wording. In other words, run-ons occur when two or more sentences are crammed into one. Run-ons can be confusing, and because of the syntax of run-ons, readers might not read run-ons with the proper **pace** or **emphasis**.

Example: My brother is nice my sister is not. [run-on]

Example: Yesterday I was packing my kids' lunches when I heard something near the garage so I grabbed a pot from the cabinet and looked out the window it was only a raccoon. [run-on]

There are several **ways to edit run-ons**, but here are three of the more common ways:

1. Place a **PERIOD** between the two independent clauses.

    My brother is nice. My sister is not.

2. Use a **SEMICOLON** between the two independent clauses.

    My brother is nice; my sister is not.

3. Use a **COMMA AND COORDINATING CONJUNCTION** (FANBOYS=for, and, nor, but, or, yet, so) between the two independent clauses.

    My brother is nice, but my sister is not.

Exercise 2.1a   Identifying Run-ons

Is my sentence a run-on?

Read your sentences and ask where a period should go. If there's no period where one is needed, you've got a run-on.

1. Adam and Eve lived in Eden it was paradise on earth

    A. This sentence is a run-on
    B. This sentence is correct

2. Because Noah was a righteous man, he was spared.

   A. This sentence is a run-on
   B. This sentence correctly joins two independent clauses with the relative pronoun *because*

3. Jonah disobeyed God he ran away and fled on a ship.

   A. This sentence is a run-on
   B. This sentence is correct

4. Moses was a prince, but he sacrificed everything in order to save the Israelites.

   A. This sentence is a run-on
   B. This sentence correctly combines two independent clauses with a comma + FANBOYS

5. God let Satan take everything from Job, but Job never lost his faith.

   A. This sentence is a run-on
   B. This sentence correctly combines two independent clauses with a comma + FANBOYS

Comma Splices

A **comma splice** occurs when writers join two independent clauses with a comma only. It's just like a run-on, except where the two independent clauses meet, there is a comma.

Example: My brother is nice, my sister is not. [splice]

Dissection: Note how there's an independent clause on *both* sides of the comma: "My brother is nice" is independent, and "my sister is not" is independent.

Comma splices often occur when writers use articles or personal or demonstrative pronouns after commas.

Example: Dad is cranky in the morning, he needs his coffee. [splice]

Dissection: Note how the personal pronoun "he" comes right after the comma.

> **Reminder**
>
> An independent clause has a subject and a verb, and can stand on its own. It's independent. It doesn't need any help. Treat independent clauses as **complete sentences**. See section 1.6 for more on clauses.

Like run-ons, comma splices can be confusing to the reader because of the way they incorrectly emphasize words and the way they distort the pace with which you want readers to read your sentences.

There are several ways to **fix a comma splice**. Here are three of the more common approaches:

1. Place a **period** between the two independent clauses (where the comma was).

    Example: My brother is nice. My sister is not.

> For more on semicolon use, see section 2.7C

2. Use a **semicolon**. Note that semicolons are for *very closely related* ideas.

    Example: My brother is nice; my sister is not.

3. Use a **comma and coordinating conjunction**. It's easy to remember these conjunctions by recalling the acronym FANBOYS (for, and, nor, but, or, yet, so).

Example: My brother is nice, but my sister is not.

Exercise 2.1b   Identifying Comma Splices

<u>Directions</u>: Circle the letter that best describes the sentence.

1. Adam and Eve lived in Eden, it was paradise on earth

   A. This sentence contains a comma splice
   B. This sentence is correct

2. Noah was a righteous man, therefore he was spared.

   A. This sentence contains a comma splice
   B. This sentence correctly combines two independent clauses with a comma + FANBOYS

> **Trouble Spot**
>
> Avoid placing a comma only before *however* and *therefore* since doing so creates comma splices. Use a semicolon before the conjunctive adverb followed by a comma when joining independent clauses (; however,).

3. Jonah disobeyed God, he ran away and fled on a ship.

   A. This sentence contains a comma splice
   B. This sentence is correct

4. Moses was a prince, but he sacrificed everything in order to save the Israelites.

   A. This sentence contains a comma splice

B. This sentence correctly combines two independent clauses with a comma + FANBOYS

5. God let Satan take everything from Job, Job never lost his faith in God.

   A. This sentence contains a comma splice
   B. This sentence is correct

Fragments

A **fragment** occurs when writers fail to create complete sentences. With few exceptions, a sentence must have a subject and verb and express a complete thought. In other words, sentences should have at least one independent clause.

   A. While driving down the street in my car with my friends. [fragment]
   B. During the summer, my brother who loves to eat hot dogs. [fragment]
   C. Aunt Mary is kind. Especially to strangers. [The sentence that begins "Especially" is a fragment]

Fragments are generally very careless errors that show a lack of revision effort. Since they tend to be incomplete ideas, they confuse readers, who, as a result of the fragment, don't understand the point of the sentence or how the ideas relate.

Note the following constructions, which, coincidentally, tend to be found where there are fragments:

1. *Who*, *whose*, *which*, *that*, and words that end *–ing* tend to create fragments.
2. Avoid beginning sentences with *especially* and *which*.

There are several ways to **fix a fragment**. Here are three of the more common approaches:

1. Add an **independent clause**.

[Revised version of A]: While driving down the street in my car with my friends, <u>I texted my girlfriend.</u>

2. **Delete** the part causing the fragment.

[Revised version of B]: During the summer, my brother loves to eat hot dogs.

3. **Combine** the fragment with a neighboring sentence by using a comma.

[Revised version of C]: <u>Aunt Mary is kind,</u> especially to strangers.

Exercise 2.1c   Identifying Fragments

<u>Directions</u>: Circle the letter that corresponds to the most accurate description of the sentence.

1. Adam and Eve, who lived in Eden and had heaven on earth.

   A. This sentence is a fragment
   B. This sentence is correct

2. Noah was a righteous man. Especially because he obeyed God.

   A. One of these sentences is a fragment
   B. These sentences are correct

3. Jonah, fleeing on a ship after he disobeyed God, eventually getting swallowed by a huge fish.

   A. This sentence is a fragment
   B. This sentence is correct

4. Moses was a prince. He sacrificed his power and status in order to save the Israelites.

   A. One of these sentences is a fragment
   B. These sentences are correct

5. God let Satan take everything. From Job.

   A. One of these sentences is a fragment
   B. These sentences are correct

Exercise 2.1d
Correcting Splices, Run-ons, and Fragments

Directions: Correct the following splices, run-ons, and fragments by using the technique requested in parentheses.

1. He is nice, she is not. (*Edit the splice by adding a **semicolon** between the independent clauses*)

   _____

   _____

_____

_____

2. My brother always calls me on my birthday I sometimes forget to call him. *(Edit the run-on by adding **comma + coordinating conjunction** between the independent clauses)*

_____

_____

_____

_____

3. Beneath the table you'll find a pair of scissors be careful because they are sharp. *(Edit the run-on by placing a **period** between the independent clauses)*

_____

_____

_____

_____

4. Texting while someone is trying to speak to you is rude I hope you never do that again. *(Edit the run-on by placing a **period** between the independent clauses)*

_____

_____

_____

_____

5. Mississippi Map turtles are native to the south they have been found as far north as Ohio. *(Edit the run-on by adding **comma + coordinating conjunction** between the independent clauses)*

_____

_____

_____

_____

6. Laurie never says hello to me when she's with the popular kids. Which annoys me. *(Fix the fragment by placing a **comma** between the dependent clause and independent clause)*

_____

_____

_____

_____

7. Pursuing my dreams with all my heart and soul. *(Add a **verb** to fix the fragment)*

_____

_____

_____

_____

8. Rico, who loves to dance and chat with the ladies. *(**Delete** the word that's causing the fragment and rewrite the sentence)*

_____

_____

_____

_____

9. I probably won't come over tonight to watch the game. Especially if you don't provide pizza and soda. *(Edit the fragment by placing a **comma** between the dependent and independent clauses)*

_____

_____

_____

_____

10. The number that you dialed is incorrect, please check the number and dial again. *(Edit the splice by inserting a **coordinating conjunction** between the independent clauses)*

_____

_____

_____

_____

Exercise 2.1e
Splices, Run-ons, and Fragments in Context

Directions: Choose the letter that corresponds to the best answer.

1. Some people never say thanks when I hold the door; which is very annoying.

   A. Replace the semicolon with a comma and combine the two sentences
   B. Replace the semicolon with a period
   C. No change

2. Two people who live upstairs from me in a spectacular penthouse apartment.

   A. Add a period after upstairs and start a new sentence with *from*
   B. Delete the word *who*
   C. No change

3. I love water sports. Such as water polo, pool basketball, and synchronized swimming.

   A. Change the period to a semicolon
   B. Replace the period with a comma and combine the two sentences
   C. No Change

4. The boy, whose coat you borrowed last week because you forgot yours.

   A. Delete the word *whose*

B. Change the period to a comma and add *is always very considerate.*

C. No change

5. Sometimes when we argue about trivial matters in front of our parents.

   A. Add a period after *matters* and start a new sentence with *in*
   B. Delete the word *when*
   C. No change

6. Not many cars were on the road I headed onto Route 25A east and then to the Sagtikos Parkway.

   A. Add a comma after *road*
   B. Delete *then*
   C. Add the word *when* after *road*

7. When the bell rang at 3:05, I entered the hallway and walked toward my locker to get my books I was in a rush.

   A. Delete *When*
   B. Place a period after *locker*
   C. Place a period after *books*

8. That happened when I was a teenager it changed me.

   A. Place a comma and the coordinating conjunction *and* after the word *teenager*
   B. Add a comma after *teenager*
   C. Place a period after *I*

9. It was March of 2011, I was on my way to the airport with my family.

   A. Add a comma after *way*
   B. Change the comma to a period
   C. Delete *my*

10. I noticed the flags hanging from everyone's flagpoles on Memorial Day everything looked so patriotic to me.

   A. Delete *everything*
   B. Place a period after *Day*
   C. Place a period after *flags*

A. Write a sentence fragment. Then correct it.

_____

_____

_____

_____

_____

B. Write a run-on. Then correct it.

_____

_____

_____

_____

_____

C. Write a comma splice. Then correct it.

_____

_____

_____

_____

_____

9

SUBJECT-VERB AGREEMENT

Subjects and verbs must **agree in number** (singular and plural). If the subject is plural, for example, the verb should be plural.

Sometimes it's hard to decipher what the subject is, especially when a <u>prepositional phrase</u> comes between subject and verb. Sometimes it's unclear if the subject is singular or plural, as is the case with sentences containing words such as *everybody*, *nobody*, and *group*. Consider the following common agreement errors and techniques for correcting them.

Example: My professor never respond to my email. [Incorrect]

The verb (*respond*) is plural; the subject (*professor*) is singular. Subject and verb don't agree.

Technique: Substitute a plural pronoun (they) for a plural subject and a singular (it) for a singular subject and place the pronoun next to the verb to test.

Technique applied: It...responds or it...respond? It... responds. [Correct]

Revised: My professor never responds to my email. [Correct]

Avoid the **common traps**:

1. For sentences with **either/or** and **neither/nor**: number is determined by the subject that is <u>closer to the verb</u>.

Example: Neither my three dogs nor your cat (is/are) going to the vet.

Answer: **is** because *cat* is closer to the verb, so *cat is going*, not cat are going.

Technique: Place the subject (cat) next to the verb.

2. Don't confuse **prepositional phrases** with subjects.

Example: The cobwebs on that wall (has/have) been there for a long time.

Answer: **have** because "on that wall" is a prepositional phrase, "wall" is not the subject. "Cobwebs" is the subject. Cobwebs <u>have been</u> there.

Technique: ~~Strike through~~ **prepositional phrases** that come between subjects and verbs so that you don't confuse the object of the preposition with the subject. The cobwebs on that wall (has/have) been there for a long time.

3. Memorize words that *appear* plural, but are in fact **singular**, such as the following: *anybody, anyone, each, everyone, everybody, nobody, no one, somebody, someone,* and the names of courses, even the ones that end in −s (physics, calculus, etc).

> **Reminder**
>
> Review sections 1.1 and 1.2 on identifying subjects, verbs, nouns, and prepositional phrases, which will remind you that not every noun is the subject.

4. Learn the words that are **usually singular**, but can be plural, depending upon your intention: *group, team, committee, class, media,* and *family.*

5. **Compound subjects** are always plural. Look for the word "and" in such instances.

Example: My aunt, who loves to ski, and my uncle, who enjoys biking, are two of the more active people I know.

Answer: The subject is compound ("aunt" and "uncle" joined by "and") so the verb must be plural (are)

Exercise 2.2a   Subject-Verb Agreement

<u>Directions</u>: Circle the verb that agrees with the subject.

1. Everybody who lives in cities (enjoys/enjoy) the nightlife.

2. The team (is/are) going to celebrate after winning the World Series.

3. After every season, the manager, along with the owners, (thanks/thank) the fans for supporting the team.

4. My uncles and aunt (argues/argue) every year at Thanksgiving.

5. Neither my brother nor my sisters (was/were) at my graduation.

6. Either the professors or the dean (has/have) been embezzling money.

7. Nobody in this house (is/are) going to get a present since the chores haven't been finished.

8. The pants I am wearing (feel/feels) too tight.

9. The eyes of the box turtle, which (is/are) often red, (distinguishes/distinguish) it from other turtles.

10. The nagging, whining, and bickering of children (makes/make) me reluctant to have children of my own.

Exercise 2.2b
Agreement Errors with Prepositional Phrases

Directions: ~~Strike through~~ the prepositional phrases that come between the subject and the verb. Then circle the verb that agrees with the subject.

> **Reminder**
> Remember tricky agreement problems: words that appear plural but aren't; parts of speech that appear like subjects, but aren't; how to handle either/or and neither/nor, and what a compound subject is.

1. The tinted windows on my car (draw/draws) the attention of police.

2. A new development of homes (is/are) going to be built in Commack, but not in Brentwood.

3. Some historians who have written about George Washington (has/have) admired the first president's decision not to serve any more than two terms.

4. Economics—the scientific study of the production, consumption, and transfer of wealth—(has/have) played a vital role in presidential elections in the twenty-first century.

5. Strategic use of weapons (was/were) instrumental in the success of the mission.

6. The freedom of birds and butterflies (is/are) something to behold and emulate.

> **Reminder**
> Review section 1.2 on identifying prepositional phrases.

7. The reptile, a cold-blooded creature with scales, (has/have) survived for more than three hundred million years.

8. He handed me a set of keys that (open/opens) every door in the building.

9. The disappearance of many ships (lead/leads) some scholars to believe that the Bermuda Triangle is a truly supernatural place.

10. The manager, along with the owners, (deserve/deserves) a great deal of credit for the team's success.

10

VERB TENSE

Tense refers to the "time" of a verb's action or being. Tense indicates when an action takes place, took place, or will take place. In English, verbs may be in one of the following six tenses: present, past, future, present perfect, past perfect, and future perfect.

Present Tense:
I drive to campus.

Past Tense:
I drove to campus yesterday.

Future Tense:
I will drive to campus tomorrow.

Present Perfect:
I have driven to campus many times in the past.

Past Perfect:
<u>I had driven</u> to campus before I realized that I forgot my book.

Future Perfect:
<u>I will have driven</u> fifty miles before I run out of gas.

Use this tense chart to learn the purposes and formations of the six tenses:

Tense	Purpose	Example	Conjugation	
present	Actions or conditions in present	She eats dinner every day.	I eat	we eat
			you eat	you eat
			he, she, it eats	they eat
past	Actions or conditions started and completed in the past	She ate lobster for dinner yesterday.	I ate	we ate
			you ate	you ate
			he, she, it ate	they ate
future	Actions or conditions occurring in future	She will eat lobster for dinner tomorrow.	I will eat	we will eat
			you will eat	you will eat
			he, she, it will eat	they will eat
present perfect	Actions or conditions started in the past and continuing to the present; repeated past actions	She has eaten lobster.	I have eaten	we have eaten
			you have eaten	you have eaten
			he, she, it has eaten	they have eaten

past perfect	Past actions or conditions that start and finish before some later past action starts	She had eaten the lobster before she felt nauseated.	I had eaten	we had eaten
			you had eaten	you had eaten
			he, she, it had eaten	they had eaten
future perfect	Future actions or conditions that start and end before some later future action starts	She will have eaten three pounds of lobster before I finish chewing my first piece.	I will have eaten	we will have eaten
			you will have eaten	you will have eaten
			he, she, it will have eaten	they will have eaten

Learn how to conjugate the verb *to be*:

Tense	Conjugation	
present	I am	we are
	you are	you are
	he, she, it is	they are
past	I was	we were
	you were	you were
	he, she, it was	they were
future	I will be	we will be
	you will be	you will be
	he, she, it will be	they will be

present perfect	I have been	we have been
	you have been	you have been
	he, she, it has been	they have been
past perfect	I had been	we had been
	you had been	you had been
	he, she, it had been	they had been
future perfect	I will have been	we will have been
	you will have been	you will have been
	he, she, it will have been	they will have been

Potential Tense Trouble Spots

Revise verbs so that they are in the **correct tense**. If you want to distinguish between two past actions, use the past perfect; if you want to indicate an action that will take place in the future, use the future.

Example: Yesterday, I *had gone* to the store. <u>Incorrect</u> use of past perfect.

Revise so that your writing doesn't **shift tenses**. A tense shift is an incorrect movement from one tense to another. These shifts can be within a sentence, in neighboring sentences, or even between paragraphs.

Example: Rick *sells* shoes at the mall during the day and *worked* security at night. <u>Tense shift</u> from present (*sells*) to past (*worked*)

Exercise 2.3a Tense Formation

Directions: Fill in the blank with the appropriate form of the verb that is parenthetically supplied in the infinitive form.

1. I _____ to school every day. (*present tense*: to drive)

2. Practicing grammar _____ me feel nauseated and dizzy. (*present tense*: to make)

3. He _____ the grass seed in early spring. (*past tense*: to plant)

4. The New York Yankees_____ the Mets in the Subway Series. (*past tense*: to defeat)

5. Heather _____ in order to feed her children. (*future tense:* to steal)

6. We _____ each other's homework during the semester. (*future tense:* to copy)

7. They _____ for me in the past. (*present perfect:* to work)

8. She _____ my friend for forty years. (*present perfect*: to be)

9. Before humans appeared, turtles _____ on earth for 200 million years. (*past perfect*: to be)

10. Lundy _____ a million dollars by the time he turned twenty. (*past perfect*: to earn)

11. You _____ long before the sun explodes. (*future perfect:* to die)

12. The semester _____ by the time you finish your paper, you slacker! (*future perfect:* to end)

Exercise 2.3b   Tense Identification

<u>Directions</u>: Identify the italicized verb by writing its corresponding tense name (present, past, future, present perfect, past perfect, future perfect) in the space provided. Use the verb tense chart at the beginning of this section for help with tense identification.

1. Marge *will have answered* your questions by the time I return. _____

2. Ava *has finished* drinking her bottle.

   _____

3. Ackerman and Lundy *have called* me several times today. _____

4. I *will give* you five dollars tomorrow.

   _____

5. Veronica *borrowed* my golf clubs.

   _____

6. The students *have prayed* for snow.

_____

7. The man *commands* respect from everyone he has met.

_____

Tense Errors

Refer to the first few pages of this section on verbs, especially the charts, to assist with the completion of the exercises on verbs.

8. Curtis Martin *will have rushed* for fifteen thousand yards by the time he retires. _____

9. The Mets *had lost* sixty games by the all-star break.

_____

10. The alien *will abduct* unsuspecting earthlings.

_____

11. Everyone in the family *believes* in you.

_____

12. I *will be* nineteen in three months.

_____

13. I *had been* his girlfriend until he cheated on me. _____

14. By next January, I *will have been* married for thirteen years. _____

Exercise 2.3c Tense Shifts and Errors

Directions: Read the following sentences. Some of the sentences contain shifts or improper uses of tense. Choose the answer that represents the most correct use of tense.

1. For the past three years, she <u>will have been</u> my friend.

    A. No Change
    B. has been
    C. is

2. Jeter <u>fields</u> the ball and threw quickly to first.

    A. No Change
    B. has fielded
    C. fielded

3. We <u>have taken</u> a class together before we met.

    A. No Change
    B. took
    C. had taken

4. After Washington was general, he <u>had served</u> as president.

    A. No Change
    B. served
    C. has served

5. I <u>will have served</u> as chair for seven years by the time I retire.

    A. No Change

B. had served
C. will serve

6. The reporter <u>has asked</u> that question a thousand times already!

   A. No Change
   B. asks
   C. had asked

7. Everyone <u>believed</u> that the surgery will be successful.

   A. No Change
   B. has believed
   C. believes

8. I <u>have defeated</u> Kulkosky many times in the past.

   A. No Change
   B. had defeated
   C. defeat

9. Before the milk spilled, she <u>had warned</u> me not to shake the table.

   A. No Change
   B. will have warned
   C. warned

10. I <u>mastered</u> verb tense by practicing for three weeks.

    A. No Change
    B. master
    C. has mastered

11

PRONOUNS

Pronoun Agreement

When you revise, make sure your pronouns **agree in number** (singular/plural) with their **antecedents** (the words they refer to).

Example: A **person** should try to do **their** best. Agreement Error.

Note how the pronoun (their) and its antecedent (a person) don't agree in number. *their* = plural; *a person* = singular.

In order to **fix the error**, revise the <u>pronoun </u>or its <u>antecedent</u>.

Edited Antecedent: People should try to do their best. (Correct revision by changing the number of the antecedent to plural.)

Edited Pronoun: A person should try to do her best. (Correct revision by changing the number of the pronoun to singular.)

Identifying and Editing Pronoun Agreement Errors

Remember some tricky pronoun agreement traps:

1. Some nouns appear plural, but are singular: *anybody*, *each*, *either*, *everybody*, *everyone*, *family*, *group*, *nobody*, *somebody*, *team.* When the group is viewed as a whole, it is singular; when it is viewed as a series of individuals, it is plural.

2. Special case A: either/or and neither/nor agreement is determined by the noun that's closer to the pronoun.

Example: Either the two privates or the <u>captain</u> is going to abandon *his* post.

Explanation: Since "captain" is closer to the pronoun than "two privates," the pronoun must agree with "captain" (singular).

3. Special case B: Some nouns, called **collective nouns**, can be singular or plural, depending on the context: *class*, *group*, *jury*, *family*, and *team*, but usually, these

words are singular. Some **indefinite pronouns** are singular: *anybody*, *anything*, *each*, etc.

Example: The *group* is going to be rewarded for *its* effort.

Explanation: Since "group" is singular, a singular pronoun ("its") is correct.

Exercise 2.4a Pronoun Agreement

Directions: The words in bold are pronouns. 1. Circle their antecedents. 2. If pronoun and antecedent agree, write **correct** in the blank; if they don't, write **incorrect**.

_____1. A person knows that it's foolish to put drugs into **their** bodies.

_____2. The group of people sitting at the bar left **their** tip under the ashtray.

_____3. Either the players or the coach will take responsibility for **their** unsportsmanlike behavior.

_____4. Everyone who lives in my house knows that **they** should help out with the chores.

_____5. A good person does not forget to say thank you, and **he** does not forget to say "please."

_____6. Both the dog and the cat shed **its** fur.

_____7. Which representative on the committee spoke **their** mind most passionately?

_____8. Every person knows that **they** must think of others' feelings

_____9. The student-teacher conference has a number of functions, but **their** main one has to do with improving the student-teacher relationship.

_____10. If Wal-Mart doesn't stay open late on Christmas Eve, **they** will lose a lot of customers.

Write a sentence that has a pronoun agreement error in which the pronoun is <u>plural</u> and the antecedent is <u>singular</u>. Circle the pronoun and its antecedent.

_____

_____

_____

_____

_____

Pronoun Case

By now, you should be aware of the mischief that pronouns can create with sentence clarity and unity; but because we rely on pronouns so much, we should be forgiving and do our best not to misuse this important part of speech. An additional aspect of pronouns that writers misunderstand is pronoun case, so when you revise, make sure your pronouns are in the correct **case** (subject, object, etc.).

This section will help you with the following pronoun case questions: Do I use *I* or *me*? *Who* or *whom*? In other words, should the pronoun be in the subject case or some other case? Basically, the answer **depends upon the verb**. If you put the pronoun next to the verb and the wording makes sense, you're probably right.

Identifying and Editing Pronoun Case Errors

Answer the following question:

Example: My mother warned my brother and _____ to stop fighting.

A. I
B. me
C. myself
D. your

> **Look Back**
> See section 1.4 for types of pronouns and their functions.

Ways to Determine Pronoun Case

1. Know the different cases of pronouns. See section 1.4.
2. Place the pronoun next to the verb. In a somebody and I/somebody and me sentence, delete the other person (leaving only the I/me). In the example above: Ask if "My mother warned I to stop?" or "My mother warned me to stop? Answer: Mother warned me. (She warned me.) What you're really asking is if the pronoun is acting on the verb (warned). In this case, no: *mother* is the subject of *warned*. Try to determine if the pronoun acts on the verb or if there is already a subject acting on the verb.
3. Use **possessive pronouns** before participles (verbs that end –*ing* such as driving, complaining).

   Example:
   She doesn't like my driving while texting.

not
She doesn't like me driving while texting.
Why? Because it's not "me" she doesn't like, but what I'm doing (texting).

4. Use **reflexive pronouns** for <u>emphasis</u> (I did the work myself!), when the subject does something <u>to/for/by/ with itself</u> (She earned the money by herself.), and, in general, when the pronoun refers to another pronoun in the sentence. Example: He can do it all by himself. Note how *himself* refers back to *He*. Reflexive pronouns **do not act alone on verbs**. Example of <u>incorrect</u> use: Myself is going to the store. Reflexive pronouns need a pronoun or noun antecedent before them to have a chance of being correct. Correct use: I myself am going to the store. Note how the reflexive pronoun is preceded by a pronoun.

Exercise 2.4b Pronoun Case

<u>Directions</u>: Using the strategies above, circle the letter that corresponds to the correct answer.

1. In order to excel on the exam, Celeste and _____ will study for at least three hours.

   A. I
   B. me
   C. myself
   D. them

2. My brother and _____ are going to the movies tonight.

A. I
B. me
C. them
D. us

3. Professor Gatti asked Bruce and _____ to stay after class because we had been so disruptive.

    A. I
    B. me
    C. we
    D. themselves

4. Kareem Abdul Jabbar spoke to my dad and _____ after the game, and he even autographed my shirt.

    A. me
    B. I
    C. we
    D. they

5. It was _____ who ate the last of the peanut M&Ms.

    A. me
    B. I
    C. her
    D. us

6. They said that it was _____ who forgot to flush, but in fact, it was _____.

    A. he…me
    B. him…her
    C. he…I
    D. myself…us

7. My uncle was angry at _____ failing to say goodbye before I left for college.

Clue for question 7

Is the uncle angry at the person or what the person did? If it's the latter (what the person did), use the possessive pronoun (my).

A. me
B. my
C. myself
D. I

8. Professor Inners, disappointed by _____ procrastinating, admonished me not to wait until the last minute before starting my drafts.

A. my
B. me
C. you
D. yourself

9. It was he _____ who completed the entire project.

A. himself
B. me
C. myself
D. theirself

10. My children can feed _____.

A. herself
B. himself
C. themselves
D. ourselves

A. Write your own pronoun case question, modeling it on any of those above. Then circle the correct answer.

_____

_____

_____

_____

_____

Pronoun Reference

When you revise, make sure your pronouns **have clear references.** Also known as ambiguous pronouns, pronouns reference errors create confusion for readers.

Example: John and Rick went to the mall, but *he* never came back. (Unclear because "he" could refer to John or Rick.)

Example: He is rude, conceited, and dishonest. *That* is why I despise him. (Unclear because "that" could refer to rude, conceited, or dishonest. It's not clear why the writer despises him.)

Try to avoid using **demonstrative** pronouns as the first or last word of a sentence because they tend to be very unclear in these locations. Demonstrative pronouns include *this, that, these*, and *those*. Find a different way to end your sentences or follow these pronouns with specific nouns. If you are going to be stubborn and use demonstrative pronouns at the end of your sentences, try to use them with their antecedents.

Example: I will not accept this. (Incorrectly ends sentence with unclear demonstrative pronoun.)

Edited: I will not accept this work. (Correctly ends with demonstrative pronoun [this] + antecedent [work], thereby eliminating the confusion.)

Exercise 2.4c   Pronoun Reference Errors

<u>Directions</u>: Circle the unclear pronoun in each sentence.

1. Jeter and Rodriguez are the best players on the team, but he is clearly the better person.

2. Donna and Jane disagreed about the proposal, but she didn't have to be so nasty while asserting her point.

3. Mom told us we didn't have to shower tonight because we were taking a road trip. This made us so excited.

4. They say that you should do unto others as you would have others do unto you.

5. It says in the newspaper that our taxes will increase again this year.

6. Professor Hunt didn't respond to my calls or return my emails, so now I'm angry because of this.

7. My ex cheats, lies, and stalks. That is why I dumped her in the first place.

8. I am going to demand a refund because they charged me twice for the same item.

9. Some people prefer Lawrence's novels, others his short stories, and still others love his poetry. I like those the best.

10. Our class has spent a lot of time on pronouns, nouns, subjects, and verbs. I hate studying them.

A. Write your own question, modeled on those above. Then circle the unclear pronoun.

_____

_____

_____

_____

_____

Pronoun Shifts

When you revise, make sure your pronouns don't shift; otherwise, sentences might prove confusing and inconsistent.

Example: Although **we** were slowly getting closer to **our** destination, **you** could see that everyone was getting frustrated.

Explanation: *we*=first person plural, *our*= first person plural, *you*=second person

Edited: Although **we** were slowly getting closer to **our** destination, **we** could see that everyone was getting frustrated.

Exercise 2.4d   Pronoun Shifts

<u>Directions</u>: Edit the sentences so that the pronouns are consistent.

1. When one studies, _____ well.

    A. you do
    B. I do
    C. one does
    D. they do

2. After we finished watching the movie, _____ felt depressed.

    A. we
    B. you
    C. one
    D. they

3. If you want to bake a delicious cake, you should follow the directions. First, however, _____ should mix the ingredients.

    A. one
    B. I
    C. they
    D. you

4. Teachers who believe in their students know that
   _____ must give students challenging assignments.

   A. they
   B. you
   C. I
   D. he

5. However much I despise grammar, I know that
   _____ must learn it in order to improve my chances
   at earning a living.

   A. one
   B. he
   C. I
   D. they

6. If a student wants help, _____ that I will be there.

   A. he or she knows
   B. one knows
   C. they know
   D. you know

7. To learn how to speak in public is an important skill
   for students. Learning to do so prepares _____ for
   so many occasions when _____ will have to speak
   to an audience.

   A. her...she
   B. me...I
   C. us...you
   D. them...they

8. When _____ converse with others, _____ should listen carefully, and think before responding.

   A. they...a person
   B. one...a person
   C. you...they
   D. we...we

9. When my father was a kid, _____ paid only five cents for a movie.

   A. you
   B. we
   C. he
   D. they

10. Some physicists and astronomers believe that _____ will eventually discover an earth-like planet, capable of sustaining life.

    A. one
    B. you
    C. themselves
    D. they

A. Write your own pronoun shift question using the questions in the exercise above as models. Then circle the correct answer.

_____

_____

_____

_____

12

PARALLELISM

Parallelism is a principle of effective writing that emphasizes **symmetry** in sentence structure. When sentences are parallel, they are concise, clear, and beautiful. Three of the more common errors in parallelism are listed below.

1. Revise so that sentences are **parallel in verb forms**, especially in infinitives and participles.

Faulty Parallelism	Nature of the Error	Corrected Version
She likes hiking, biking, and to ski.	Mixes infinitive (to) and participle (-ing)	She likes hiking, biking, and skiing.
I like to sing, to dance, and swimming is also fun.	Mixes infinitive (to) and participle (-ing)	I like to sing, dance, and swim.

2. Revise so that sentences are **parallel in their comparisons**.

Faulty Parallelism	Nature of the Error	Corrected Version
My love for music is greater than baseball.	Compares love for music to baseball instead of comparing love to love.	My love for music is greater than my love for baseball.
Da Vinci's Mona Lisa is more famous than Van Gogh.	Compares fame of artwork to fame of artist.	Da Vinci is more famous than Van Gogh.

3. Revise so that sentences are **parallel in voice (active and passive)**.

Faulty Parallelism	Nature of the Error	Corrected Version
He came, he saw, and it was conquered by him.	Shifts from active (came) to passive (conquered by him)	He came, he saw, and he conquered.
Jones bought a new hat, exited the store, and his car was driven away.	Shifts from active (bought) to passive (was driven)	Jones bought a new hat, exited the store, and drove away.

Look Ahead

For more on active and passive voice, see section 3.2

Exercise 2.5a Parallel Structure

<u>Directions</u>: Choose the answer that corresponds to the most parallel version of the sentence.

1. Larry Bird was a clutch shooter, ferocious rebounder, and he was also a skilled passer.

   A. Larry Bird was a clutch shooter, he rebounded ferociously, passed skillfully.
   B. Larry Bird was a clutch shooter, ferocious rebounder, and skilled passer.
   C. No change

2. By practicing free throws, studying film, and when he showed determination, Magic Johnson transformed from a great player to a legendary one.

   A. Through free throw practice, film study, and determination, Magic Johnson transformed from a great player to a legendary one
   B. By practicing free throws, studying film, and determination, Magic Johnson transformed from a great player to a legendary one
   C. No change

3. Some say that Michael Jordan's talent was greater than Lebron James.

   A. Some say that Michael Jordan's talent was greater than Lebron James' talent
   B. Some say that Michael Jordan is greater than Lebron James' talent.
   C. No change

4. Massachusetts is the home of the Boston Celtics and the Basketball Hall of Fame.

    A. Massachusetts is the home of the Boston Celtics, and the Basketball Hall of Fame is also there.
    B. The Boston Celtics reside in Massachusetts, so does the Basketball Hall of Fame, which is in Springfield.
    C. No change

5. During the 1961–62 season, Oscar Robertson averaged a triple double, Wilt Chamberlain averaged fifty points and twenty-five rebounds, and more than thirty points per game were earned, typically, by Jerry West.

    A. During the 1961–62 season, Oscar Robertson averaged a triple double, Wilt Chamberlain averaged fifty points and twenty-five rebounds, and Jerry West averaged more than thirty points per game.
    B. During the 1961–62 season, Oscar Robertson averaged a triple double, Wilt Chamberlain collecting fifty points and twenty-five rebounds, and more than thirty points per game were earned, typically, by Jerry West.
    C. No change

6. Four presidents have been assassinated: Lincoln, Garfield, McKinley, and Kennedy was as well.

    A. Four presidents have been assassinated: Lincoln, Garfield, McKinley, and Kennedy.
    B. Four presidents have been assassinated: Lincoln, Garfield, Mckinley, and so was Kennedy.
    C. No Change

7. There have been several failed presidential assassination attempts: a misfire spared Andrew Jackson, a speech saved Teddy Roosevelt, a woman saved Franklin Delano Roosevelt, a secret service agent rescued Harry Truman, and Ronald Reagan was saved by doctors.

   A. There have been several failed presidential assassination attempts: Andrew Jackson was spared by a misfire, Teddy Roosevelt was saved by a speech, Franklin Delano Roosevelt was saved by a woman, a secret service agent rescued Harry Truman, and Ronald Reagan was saved by doctors.
   B. There have been several failed presidential assassination attempts: a misfire spared Andrew Jackson, a speech saved Teddy Roosevelt, a woman saved Franklin Delano Roosevelt, a secret service agent rescued Harry Truman, and doctors saved Ronald Reagan.
   C. No change

8. Congress' popularity is low because of its lack of ethics, and since they are not very high on competence.

   A. Congress's popularity is low because of its lack of ethics and lack of competence.
   B. Congress's popularity is low because it lacks ethics and doesn't do its job well.
   C. No change

9. As of 2014, there were 100 members of the Senate and 435 members of the House.

   A. As of 2014, the Senate consisted of 100 members and there are 435 members in the House.

B. As of 2014, the Senate consisted of 100 members and there were, in House, 435 members serving.
C. No change

10. Supreme Court Justice Hugo Black was a Klansman, and Senator Robert Byrd and President Harry Truman were also in the Ku Klux Klan.

A. President Harry Truman, Supreme Court Justice Hugo Black, and Senator Robert Byrd were Klansmen.
B. President Harry Truman, Justice Hugo Black was in the Klan, and even Senator Robert Byrd was a Klansman.
C. No change

A. Write a sentence that is *not* parallel in **verb form**.

_____

_____

_____

_____

B. Write a sentence that is *not* parallel in **comparison**.

_____

_____

_____

_____

C. Write a sentence that is *not* parallel in **voice**.

_____

_____

_____

_____

13

MODIFIERS

Modifiers are words or phrases that describe, modify, or add information about another part of a sentence. Usually functioning as adjectives or adverbs, modifiers can create confusion if they are not placed in the proper location. The key principle of modifiers is that the placement or omission of words can affect how the reader interprets your writing.

Place modifiers **as close as possible to the words they describe**. Make sure modifiers clearly modify the words they're describing. Be aware that where you place words affects the meaning of the words around them.

Key Modifier Principle: Word Order Alters Meaning

Each of the sentences in A, B, and C is correct, but note how moving one word ("only") alters the meaning:

1. I study on Saturdays only. [Implication is that Saturday is the only day the author studies]

2. I only study on Saturdays. [Implication is that the author does nothing but study on Saturdays: no work, no t.v.—not even a bath]

3. Only I study on Saturdays. [Implication is that author is the only person who studies on Saturdays; nobody else does]

Examples of Modifier Errors

1. The scientist mixed the chemicals wearing a lab coat and goggles.

Note how the sentence above seems to suggest that the chemicals are wearing the lab coat and goggles. Those words (*lab coat* and *goggles*) should be next to *scientist*.

Possible edits:

A. Wearing a lab coat and goggles, the scientist mixed the chemicals.

B. The scientist, wearing a lab coat and goggles, mixed the chemicals.

2. Dressed in a Santa suit, my nephews and nieces didn't recognize me.

Note how the sentence above seems to suggest that the nephews and nieces are dressed in a Santa suit. Whoever is dressed in the suit should immediately follow the comma.

Possible edits:

A. Dressed in a Santa suit, I wasn't recognized by my nieces and nephews.

B. Because I was dressed in a Santa suit, I wasn't recognized by my nieces and nephews.

Exercise 2.6a   Modifier Errors

<u>Directions</u>: Select the choice that corresponds to the best modifier placement.

1. Among the greatest bands of all time, people appreciate the Beatles for their lyrics, melodies, and harmonies.

   A. The Beatles, whose lyrics, melodies, and harmonies are appreciated by people.
   B. Among the greatest bands of all time, the Beatles are appreciated for their lyrics, melodies, and harmonies.
   C. No Change

2. ACDC's Angus Young performs heavy metal music wearing a schoolboy outfit.

   A. Wearing a schoolboy outfit, Angus Young performs heavy metal music.
   B. Wearing a schoolboy outfit, heavy metal music is performed by ACDC's Angus Young.
   C. No Change

3. Fleetwood Mac's *Rumors* and Pink Floyd's *Dark Side of the Moon* are among the greatest selling rock albums ever.

   A. Among the greatest selling rock albums ever, Pink Floyd and Fleetwood Mac made *Rumors* and *Dark Side of the Moon*.

B. Selling millions of albums, Pink Floyd's *Dark Side of the Moon* and Fleetwood Mac's *Rumors* include great music.
C. No Change

4. Plagued by drug addiction, alcohol took the lives of Jimi Hendrix, Jim Morrison, and Janis Joplin.

   A. Plagued by drug addiction, Jimi Hendrix, Jim Morrison, and Janis Joplin died from alcohol abuse.
   B. Plagued by drug addiction, alcohol abuse killed Jimi Hendrix, Jim Morrison, and Janis Joplin.
   C. No Change

5. Dying very young, aviation accidents killed Buddy Holly, Otis Redding, and Stevie Ray Vaughn.

   A. Dying very young in aviation accidents, Buddy Holly, Otis Redding, and Stevie Ray Vaughn.
   B. Buddy Holly, Otis Redding, and Stevie Ray Vaughn died very young in aviation accidents.
   C. No Change

6. Attempting to buzz Ozzy Osbourne's tour bus, after the wing clipped the bus guitarist Randy Rhoads crashed his plane.

   A. Attempting to buzz Ozzy Osbourne's tour bus, guitarist Randy Rhoads crashed his plane after its wing clipped the bus.
   B. Clipping its wing against Ozzy Osbourne's tour bus, guitarist Randy Rhoads crashed his plane and died.
   C. No Change

7. Known as the "Fab Four," the Beatles consisted of George Harrison, Paul McCartney, John Lennon, and Ringo Starr.

   A. Known as the "Fab Four," there were four men in the Beatles: George Harrison, Paul McCartney, John Lennon, and Ringo Starr.
   B. The Beatles, known as the "Fab Four," consisting of four men.
   C. No Change

8. With a cigarette stuck between his guitar strings, Keith Richard's solo rocked the Garden.

   A. With a cigarette stuck between his guitar strings, Keith Richard's solo was rocking.
   B. With a cigarette stuck between his guitar strings, Keith Richards rocked the Garden with a ripping solo.
   C. No Change

9. Billy Joel's roadie assured him that his microphone would work before the concert started.

   A. Before the concert started, Billy Joel's roadie assured him that the microphone would work.
   B. Having assured him that it would work, Billy Joel and his roadie were ready before the concert started.
   C. No Change

10. Neil Young sang that "rock n' roll will never die" touring in 1979.

   A. Neil Young, sang that "rock n' roll will never die" while touring in 1979.

B. While touring in 1979, Neil Young sang that "rock n' roll will never die."

C. No Change

Exercise 2.6b More Modifier Errors

<u>Directions:</u> Use the words in parentheses to fix the modifier errors. You may have to slightly alter the wording in a few sentences in order to correct the errors.

Example: Believing his daughter to be trustworthy, permission was given for her to stay out late. (father)

Edited version: <u>Believing his daughter to be trustworthy, the father gave his daughter permission to stay out late.</u>

1. Protected by thick skin and sharp reflexes, the unique characteristics enabled it to kill the cobra. (mongoose)

_____

_____

_____

_____

2. Like most people, companionship is a desire of horses. (horses)

_____

_____

_____

_____

3. Because their shells are hinged, complete enclosure is possible. (box turtles)

_____

_____

_____

_____

4. Camouflaging their skin, remaining still, and sacrificing their tails, the ability to avoid predators has evolved in lizards. (lizards).

_____

_____

_____

_____

5. Detecting sounds and smells that humans can't, barks and growls frequently were made in response to these stimuli. (dogs)

_____

_____

_____

_____

6. Hoping that someone would return his lost kitty, a reward was offered by the owner.

_____

_____

7. Exhausted from the Iditarod, the veterinarian prescribed rest and vitamins. (the sled dog)

8. Surviving harsh winters in the mud of a frozen pond, oxygen is used efficiently by turtles throughout the winter. (turtles)

9. To discourage predators, a malodorous musky scent is emitted by garter snakes.

10. Aware that the earth has had periods of global warming and global cooling long before people existed,

an awareness of climate history is encouraged in the debates about the role of human-caused climate change. (scientists)

_____

_____

_____

_____

A. Write a sentence with a modifier error and then correct it.

_____

_____

_____

_____

_____

14

PUNCTUATION

Punctuation helps writers to **separate information** for readers, shows readers how to read at the right **pace**, enables writers to **emphasize key ideas**, and even guides readers to emulate the correct **tone**. For those grammar nerds who love humorous depictions of the important role of punctuation, read *Eats, Shoots, and Leaves* or consider the following example about the effects of grammar on the meaning of a sentence:

Can you tell how profoundly the comma affects the meaning of the following sentences?

1. Let's eat mom.
2. Let's eat, mom.

Which sentence is punctuated in a way that cannibals would enjoy? Which would moms prefer? Whether you're a cannibal or a mom, or neither, punctuation is crucial for helping your reader to see relationships between words in a sentence, for guiding the reader to read your sentences with the rhythm you intended, and for helping with the emphasis of words and ideas.

In order to write and read well, you must be able to identify some key marks of punctuation and understand how to interpret them. Several types of punctuation are listed below, but this chapter will focus on commas, semicolons, colons, parentheses, dashes, and apostrophes.

Comma	,
Semicolon	;
Colon	:
Parentheses	( )
Dash	—
Apostrophe	'
Period	.
Exclamation point	!
Question mark	?
Ellipsis	…

Commas

One of the more common marks of punctuation is the **comma**. Commas produce clarity by separating information. Commas also help writers to establish pace.

Usually, less punctuation is preferable to more punctuation, but there are five situations in which you should use commas.

1. Use a comma between elements <u>in a list</u>.

My favorite sports are football, baseball, and basketball.

2. Use a comma where an independent clause (complete sentence) <u>meets</u> a dependent clause (incomplete sentence).

Although I worked hard, I lost my job.

3. Use a comma between independent clauses joined by a <u>coordinating conjunction</u> (for, and, nor, but, or, yet, so).

Dogs are very loyal, but they also bark and bite.

4. Use a comma to set off <u>appositive phrases and nonessential information.</u> (The sentence below would be complete and clear were that information between commas deleted.)

Keith Hernandez, the greatest defensive first baseman in history, retired after the 1990 season.

5. Use a comma between *multiple adjacent adjectives.*

He is a dishonest, vile man.

There is a subjective component to commas as well. Sometimes, for stylistic reasons, and to control pace, writers place commas where **pauses** are needed. So if you think a pause is necessary, use a comma, but be careful not to overuse commas because they can break the rhythm of your writing. And always avoid the comma splice (for a review of comma splices, see section 2.1).

Note: Commas almost never appear before *because.*

Exercise 2.7a   Comma Rules

<u>Directions:</u> Identify which of the above rules (1–5) describes the comma use in each sentence.

Example: I don't like grammar, but I will study it anyway. <u>#3</u>

1. If you won't apologize, I will end you. _____

2. Remember to floss, brush, and rinse in order to keep your teeth and gums healthy. _____

3. Felix is a neat freak, but Oscar is a slob. _____

4. Stradlater, Holden Caulfield's roommate at Pencey Prep, is a vain kid and a secret slob. _____

5. Derek Jeter, the Yankees all-time hits leader, may very well be the greatest short stop ever. _____

6. Hank Aaron is among the top five players in home runs, hits, runs batted in, and runs scored. _____

7. Complaining about homework, whining about tests, and not paying attention in class are just a few of the more annoying characteristics of our least favorite students. _____

8. Since you didn't revise, you can't earn a high grade on the essay. _____

9. The student exceeded the absence limit, so she will not pass the class. _____

10. Commas are frustrating, confusing marks of punctuation. _____

Exercise 2.7b Commas in Context

<u>Directions</u>: Select the response that corresponds to the best use of the comma.

1. Even though I want to hang out I'm staying home to practice my grammar.

   A. Add a comma after *out*
   B. Add a comma after *though*

2. My mother couldn't attend my poetry recitation, because she was ill.

   A. Remove the comma before *because*
   B. Add a comma after *because*

3. My brothers, and my sister will be coming to Thanksgiving dinner.

   A. Add a comma after *coming*
   B. Remove the comma after *brothers*

4. July, the warmest month of the year is also the month of my birth.

   A. Remove the comma after *July*
   B. Add a comma after *year*

5. Everyone wants to go to Disney the fun capital of the world.

    A. Add a comma after *Disney*
    B. Add a comma after *capital*

6. My favorite rides at Disney are Space Mountain, Splash Mountain and the Haunted House.

    A. Add a comma after *Disney*
    B. Add a comma before *and*

7. The bog turtle, the smallest turtle in the world, thrives in the boggy areas of the Northeast United States.

    A. Delete the comma after *world*
    B. No change

8. If you want to find a snapping turtle look near the bottom of the pond.

    A. Add a comma after *bottom*
    B. Add a comma after *turtle*

9. Frogs tend to be more aquatic than toads, but frogs will occasionally come on land to hunt insects.

    A. Delete the comma before *but*
    B. No change

10. Use commas between dependent and independent clauses, and to separate elements in a list.

    A. Delete the comma after *clauses*

B. Add a comma before and after the *and* that's between *independent* and *dependent*

Semicolons

Semicolons act as periods, but they establish relationships between two independent clauses (complete sentences) that are **much more closely related** than normal sentences. If periods go between sentences that are in the same family, semicolons go between twins.

A useful way to check if a semicolon is appropriate is to see if the ideas on each side of the semicolon point to each other.

Example: John never says please; Jane always does.

Note how the ideas on each side of the semicolon (saying please) speak to each other.

When To Use Semicolons

There are primarily two instances in which you should use a semicolon:

1. To separate <u>closely related</u> independent clauses.

Example: Travis Piazza is my friend; Anna Grishman isn't.

2. Before <u>conjunctive adverbs</u> that connect independent clauses.

Example: We didn't study; instead, we watched movies and ordered Dominos.

Examples of conjunctive adverbs: *accordingly, furthermore, moreover, similarly, also, hence, namely, still, anyway, however, nevertheless, then, besides, incidentally, thereafter, certainly, indeed, nonetheless, therefore, consequently, instead, now, thus, likewise, otherwise, undoubtedly, and meanwhile.*

Note this:
1. Check for **fragments** when using semicolons.
2. When in doubt, use a **period,** not a semicolon.

Semicolon Use and Misuse

1. Ingrid is nice; my father is nicer.
   Correct (very close relationship)

2. During the summer; Kirby studies.
   Incorrect (fragment)

3. Today is Saturday; I love summer vacation.
   Incorrect (no close relationship)

4. Yesterday, during the morning; I ate breakfast.
   Incorrect (during=fragment)

5. Ackerman is a good man; his mother is a salesperson.
   Incorrect (no close relationship)

Exercise 2.7c   Semicolon Use

<u>Directions</u>: Choose the letter that corresponds to the correct answer.

1. My brother is a great guy; my cousin is not.

    A. Change the semicolon to a comma
    B. Sentence correctly uses a semicolon between closely-related independent clauses

2. Brightly-colored snakes tend to be venomous; some snakes live in the water.

    A. Change the semicolon to a period because the independent clauses aren't closely related
    B. Sentence correctly uses a semicolon between closely-related independent clauses

3. The ancient Egyptians advanced our understanding of math; the ancient Greeks advanced our knowledge of philosophy.

    A. Change the semicolon to a comma
    B. Sentence correctly uses a semicolon between closely-related independent clauses

4. Insulation keeps houses cooler in the summer and; warmer in the winter.

    A. Delete the semicolon
    B. Sentence correctly uses a semicolon between closely-related independent clauses

5. I love partying on Thursdays because; the bars are less crowded.

   A. Delete the semicolon because it creates a fragment
   B. Sentence correctly uses a semicolon between closely-related independent clauses

6. Some people respond to my emails; others do not.

   A. Change the semicolon to a period
   B. Sentence correctly uses a semicolon between closely-related independent clauses

7. If you want to do well on the test, study; every night and visit the professor during office hours.

   A. Delete the semicolon because it creates a fragment
   B. Sentence correctly uses a semicolon between closely-related independent clauses

8. In the winter; I love to drink hot chocolate and to eat warm pudding.

   A. Delete the semicolon because it creates a fragment
   B. Sentence correctly uses a semicolon between closely-related independent clauses

9. Writing essays is very difficult; my sister is a good writer.

   A. Change the semicolon to a period since the ideas are not very closely related.
   B. Sentence correctly uses a semicolon between closely-related independent clauses

10. I don't think he meant to hurt your feelings; however, I do think he can be cruel at times.

   A. Change the semicolon to a comma
   B. Sentence correctly uses a semicolon before an adverb that joins independent clauses

Colons

Colons, usually preceded by an <u>independent clause</u>, should be used in the following instances:

1. To introduce a <u>list</u>.

Example: There are three reasons I won't marry you: you're cruel, unforgiving, and a little ugly.

2. Before an <u>explanation</u>, <u>example</u>, or a phrase that <u>logically</u> follows.

Example: Professor Jones can be frustrating: he doesn't respond to emails or return papers in a timely fashion.

3. To <u>introduce a quote</u>.

Example: In 1987, President Reagan said the following: "Mr. Gorbachev, tear down this wall."

Exercise 2.7d Colon Use

<u>Directions:</u> The following sentences require colons. Place them where they belong.

1. I dislike you for the following reasons you're dishonest, rude, and cheap.

2. Everything I've ever learned has led me to the following conclusion we have to suffer to achieve our dreams.

3. As a father, I have one goal to love my children with all my heart.

4. My life can be summed up by Tennyson's quote "Theirs not to reason why, theirs but to do and die."

5. Since I've been fumbling the ball so much, Coach has created a nickname for me Oil Hands.

6. Karen's point couldn't be clearer stop whining and do your job!

7. You know exactly what he will say if you ask him for help "I'm too busy."

8. There are three keys to success on a writing assignment read the directions, revise the paper, and submit it on time.

9. For the past ten years, we've discussed only one subject *your* feelings.

10. If you turn to page seven, you'll see the key quote "Share your joys, but not your pains."

Dashes and Parentheses

Use **parentheses** for non-essential information and for inside jokes. Use them to de-emphasize.

Example: Three weeks ago (it may have been four) we spoke about this matter.

Use the **dash** to emphasize information.

Example: He's a great kid—the greatest I've ever met.

Use a dash to show interrupted thoughts or speech.

Example:
"I would like you to—"
"Shut up?"
"—please be quiet."

The **double dash** is similar to parentheses in one regard: one can delete what's between two dashes and parentheses and the sentence should make sense.

Example: John—the cranky man right there—never paid me back.

If you delete "the cranky man right there," the sentence makes sense: John never paid me back.

Example: If you really want to (but I hope you don't) go, then go!

If you delete "but I hope you don't go," the sentence makes sense: If you really want to go, then go!

Exercise 2.7e Dashes and Parentheses

<u>Directions 1–5:</u> Examine the information in italics to determine whether to use dashes or parentheses. Then place either dashes or parentheses where needed.

1. My sister the kindest person I've ever met said she's going to give me her old car when she buys a new one. Emphasize *the kindest person I've ever met.*

2. My brother who also was born in July wants to go to a Knicks game to celebrate our birthday. Deemphasize *who also was born in July.*

3. If you really want to know how I feel about my mother I hope you don't, ask me when I'm in a better mood. Deemphasize *I hope you don't.*

4. Bring me a ratchet and a socket the 12mm socket that's right there on the table. Emphasize *the 12mm socket that's right there on the table.*

5. She kept her promise for the first time ever to pay me back. Deemphasize *for the first time ever.*

<u>Directions 6–10</u>: Decide whether to use dashes or parentheses and then place them where they belong.

6. "Please don't go. Wait! Come ba."

7. The team which I don't root for by the way appeared dejected after losing a fifth straight game.

8. The McKeever family members are broke they don't have a cent to their name.

9. When she returned my call she said it took so long because she lost my number, she seemed to think I owed her something.

10. Thursdays as I've told you many times aren't good days for me to meet.

Apostrophes

The apostrophe is primarily used in the following cases: (1) to show someone or something has or possesses something and (2) to show contraction/omission of letters.

<u>Has/possesses:</u>
Rick's ball is bouncy. (Rick owns/has the ball)

<u>Contraction:</u>
I don't like you. (don't contracted from *do* and *not*)

To determine if you need to form the possessive, rearrange the words as an "of the" phrase.

Example: the boy's hat = the hat of the boy
Example: three days' journey = journey of three days

Another way to determine whether you need an apostrophe is to see if you can **substitute a possessive pronoun** (his, her, its, their) for the noun. If you can, you *need* the apostrophe.

Example: the boy's hat = his hat
Example: my library's policy = its policy

Tricky Apostrophe Concepts

1. Distinguish between *it's* and *its*, *who's* and *whose*. It's = it is (it's a contraction).
    There is no such word as its'. *Its* is possessive, like *his* or *hers*. *Who's* is a contraction of *who is* and *whose* shows possession (whose ball is that?)

2. Distinguish between plural and possessive. Three teachers live down the street = plural (more than one teacher). The three teachers' houses reek = possessive (more than one of the teachers has/possesses a reeking house).

3. Some words form their plural irregularly. In most cases, we add —s or —es to indicate plural. Singular words such as *child* and *woman* become *children* and *women*.

4. Never use an apostrophe in a possessive pronoun (his, our, their) to show possession. These words exist to show possession, so don't add apostrophes to them.

Example: Her's = Incorrect. *Her =Correct*

5. It's standard *not* to use apostrophes next to words such as cds or next to multiple letters (there are three ps in the words pepper). So don't use apostrophes here since you are showing plural, *not* possessive. You should, however, use apostrophes when abbreviating dates. 1968 = '68. 2021 = '21

Exercise 2.7f Apostrophe Use

Directions: (1) Place apostrophes if they are needed in italicized words and (2) In the blanks, indicate if the word is plural, possessive, plural and possessive, a contraction, or a possessive pronoun that needs no apostrophe.

Example: My three *turtles'* shells look healthy. <u>Plural and possessive</u>.

1. I have three *cousins.* _____

2. My *noses* shape and size bother me.
   _____

3. The three *dogs* bowls are empty. _____

4. Aunt Montemurro thinks there are two *bs* in embarrass, but there is only one. _____

5. I *cant* finish my dinner because I foolishly ate dessert first. _____

6. The *womens* restroom, located on the third floor, is accessible by elevator. _____

7. *Elaines brothers* condition has worsened.

   _____

8. This *sports* biggest problem is extremely long and boring games. _____

9. That book isn't mine; *its* hers. _____

10. *Youll* have to wait for Donna's decision before you consider moving forward. _____

11. That mistake was *hers*, not mine. _____

12. Two of my *friends* own houses, but the rest of my friends rent. _____

13. *Its* nose is warm: that's why I know my dog is ill.

    _____

14. Four hours ago I called you and left a message, but you still *havent* called me back. _____

15. An *apostrophes* use is sometimes hard to determine.

    _____

Exercise 2.7g   More Apostrophes

Directions: Circle the letter that corresponds to the best answer.

1. Its not smart to wait until youve failed a class to ask for help.

   A. Add an apostrophe before the s in *its* and before the v in *youve*
   B. Add an apostrophe before the v in *youve*
   C. No change

2. The childrens' sneakers no longer fit.

   A. Move the apostrophe to before the s in *childrens* and add an apostrophe after the s in *sneakers*
   B. Move the apostrophe to before the s in *childrens*
   C. No change

3. I could of been a contender when I was in my prime in the 1970s.

   A. Change *could of* to *could've*
   B. Add an apostrophe before the s in *1970s*
   C. No change

4. I sold twenty CDs, earning over seventy dollars.

   A. Add an apostrophe before the s *CDs*
   B. Add an apostrophe before the s in *dollars*
   C. No change

5. The summer of 69 included the best days of my life.

    A. Add an apostrophe before the s *days*
    B. Add an apostrophe before the 6 in *69*
    C. No change

6. My ex-girlfriend loves the song "Dont you forget about me," but I happen to think that the songs' lyrics are cliché.

    A. Add an apostrophe before the t in *Dont* and move the apostrophe from after the final s to before the final -s in *songs*.
    B. Add an apostrophe before the t in *Dont*
    C. No change

7. Mom's friends daughters car is a hot black Prius.

    A. Add an apostrophe before the s *friends* and after the s in *Prius*
    B. Add an apostrophe before the s in *friend*s and before the s in *daughters*
    C. No change

8. The womens' restroom is on the left at the end of the hall.

    A. Move the apostrophe in *womens'* to before the s
    B. Delete the apostrophe in *womens'*
    C. No change

9. The swimming pool's pH is perfect.

    A. Delete the apostrophe in *pool's*
    B. Add an apostrophe before *is*
    C. No change

10. Its' not easy to determine who's ball it is.

    A. Change *who's* to *whose*

    B. Change *Its'* to *It's* and *who's* to *whose*

    C. No change

15

EASILY CONFUSED WORDS

When you revise, make sure you've used the right word, not its homophone, or some close, but distorted version of the word. Spell checker and grammar checker won't catch many of these usage errors, especially when you correctly spell the wrong word. And if you misspell a word, spell check will offer you a substitute, but you should use a dictionary to **confirm that the substitute is the right word**, not just a correctly-spelled word that resembles the word you're looking for. If you have any doubts about the word, consult a dictionary, which will help you to distinguish between easily confused words.

List of Some Easily Confused Words

affect/effect
less/fewer
there/their/they're
principal/principle
its/it's

then/than
accept/except
loose/lose
your/you're
throughout/threw out
who/which
who/whom
definitely/defiantly
between/among

Notes about Easily Confused Words

1. Use a **dictionary** if you're confused. Don't rely on spell checker or grammar checker since it usually indicates whether the word is correctly spelled, not correctly used.

2. **Who and Whom**. Who=a subject pronoun, so treat it like a he/they. Whom=an object pronoun, so treat it like him/them. Substitute *he* for *who* and *him* for *whom* and place the substitute next to the verb and you'll be able to see which is correct. An easy way to find the correct answer is to turn the who/whom clause into a question as in the examples below.

Example: He is the one (who/whom) I love. I love *him* or I love *he*? Clearly, *him* is correct because I is the subject and him is the object of the verb *love*.

Example: (Who/whom) wrote the novel? Find the verb (*wrote*) and place he/him next to it. *Him* wrote the novel or *he* wrote the novel? *He wrote the novel* is correct, so use *who*, not *whom*.

3. **Less and fewer.** Most grocery stores get this one wrong. Less refers to quantity and fewer refers to number. If you're asking how many, it's fewer. If you're asking how much, it's less.

Example: I have fewer than ten friends or less than ten friends? Are you asking how much friends or how many? *How many*, so the answer is *fewer than ten friends.*

4. For most **easily confused words with apostrophes**, remember that they are usually contractions, so say the two words out in their entirety. Don't say *it's*; say *it is*. Don't say *who's*; say *who is*.

5. **Who, which, that**. If you're referring to people, use **who**, not **which or that,** which refer to non-humans or groups.

6. With **then and than**, recall that then is for sequencing. *Then* and *time* both have the letter e. *Than* is for comparison. Both *than* and *comparison* have the letter a.

7. **There** has the word *here* in it, so it refers to place. Use *there* with the verb to be (there is, there was). **They're** is a contraction of they + are. **Their** indicates possession (their dog, their house).

8. There are no such phrases such as ~~would of~~, ~~might of~~, or ~~could of~~. It's would've (contraction of would + have),

might've (contraction of might + have), and could've (contraction of could + have).

9. **Affect** means influence; **effect** means result.

10. **Between and among**. Use *between* for two entities and *among* for more than two entities.

Examples: A wall exists between the two of us. Among the three of us, Smedley is the most intelligent.

Exercise 2.8a Easily Confused Words

<u>Directions:</u> Circle the appropriate word in each sentence. Feel free to use a dictionary.

1. She (should of/should've) referred to a dictionary to avoid confusion.

2. I (might've/might of) been the one who forgot to flush the toilet.

3. Is (you're/your) house on Main Street or Maine Street?

4. I hope (your/you're) right about her integrity.

5. I answered all of the questions (accept/except) the last one.

6. Will you (accept/except) the flowers, or am I going to have to buy you a more expensive make-up gift?

7. First I studied; (then/than) I hung out with my friends.

8. He is a better person (then/than) I am.

9. Yesterday, one of my friends, Henry Hunderfunde, (who/whom) came from Germany, told me about his shameful lineage with Nazi grandparents.

10. I want to know (who/whom) you've been texting and calling at three in the morning!

11. He is on a team (who/that) tends to excel every year.

12. She is the person (who/that) found my lost wallet.

13. I can't believe that you (throughout/threw out) the tickets to the Broadway show. They cost me $250. Darn it!

14. (Throughout/Threw out) my life, I've been puzzled by the distinction between less and fewer.

15. If I had eaten (less/fewer) dinner, I would have (less/fewer) calories to burn.

16. There are more PhDs on our faculty, but (less/fewer) good teachers.

17. (Their/They're/There) is going to be a gathering at (their/they're/there) house tonight.

18. I hope that (their/they're/there) not upset about my failure to be (their/they're/there) on time.

19. I hope you don't (loose/lose) your mind.

20. Your laces are (loose/lose). Tie them so that you don't trip.

21. Are you a person of (principal/principle)?

22. The (principal/principle) reason we chose you as (principal/principle) of the school is that you have (principals/principles).

23. (It's/Its) a rash that is likely the result of a tick bite or bed bugs.

24. I hope that (it's/its) paws haven't been injured by that broken glass.

25. He is (defiantly/definitely) not allowed to hang out with us.

26. She has been (definitely/defiantly) refusing to follow the company policies.

27. What values have been transmitted (between/among) those two generations of Americans?

28. David, (between/among) the greatest of all students, studied late into the night in order to earn good grades.

29. How were you (affected/effected) by the storm?

30. What will be the (affect/effect) if you don't do as you're told?

16

CAPITALIZING TITLES

Which words in a title should be capitalized? Here is another instance in which it's crucial to know parts of speech in order to write correctly. If you don't know what a preposition or an article is, then you probably won't know how to correctly capitalize your titles. Follow these principles for capitalization and you won't disgrace yourself or your country!

1. Capitalize the **first and last word** of a title and subtitle. Always!

Consider the following examples:

A. "Ode to the West Wind"
B. *A War Imagined: The First World War and English Culture* (first and last word of subtitle, after the colon, are capitalized)
C. *Bleak House*

2. Do *not* capitalize prepositions, articles, or coordinating conjunctions...unless they are the **first or last word** of a title or subtitle.

Consider the following examples:

A. *Of Mice and Men.* ["Of" = preposition, but capitalized because it's the first word]
B. *War and Peace.* [Conjunction "and" is in the middle]
C. *"Ode to the West Wind."* [Preposition "to" and article "the" are not capitalized when not in first or last position]

* Review

See section 1.2 for a list of prepositions and 1.7 for coordinating conjunctions. Articles include *a, an,* and *the.*]

3. Capitalize **all major words** [nouns, verbs, adjectives, adverbs, pronouns] whether they are first, last, or in the middle.

Consider the following examples:

A. *An American Tragedy.* [American = adjective]
B. *Works of Theodore Dreiser* [Theodore = noun]
C. *Complete Works of the Brontes.* [Preposition "of" and article "the" not capitalized when not in 1st or last position]

Exercise 2.9a Capitalizing Titles

<u>Directions:</u> Circle the letter that corresponds to the title that is correctly capitalized.

1. A. *Life In A Shell*
   B. *Life in a Shell*

2. A. *The works of hawthorne*
   B. *The Works of Hawthorne*

3. A. "A Letter to My Future Self"
   B. "A Letter to my Future Self"

4. A. "Humans Under The Microscope: an Analysis of *Gulliver's Travels*"
   B. "Humans under the Microscope: An Analysis of *Gulliver's Travels*"

5. A. "Misadventures At Adventureland"
   B. "Misadventures at Adventureland"

6. A. "Slavery's Impact On The Civil War"
   B. "Slavery's Impact on the Civil War"

7. A. *The federalist papers*
   B. *The Federalist Papers*

8. A. "Over my head: my struggles with basketball and college"
   B. "Over My Head: My Struggles with Basketball and College"

9. A. "A Trippin' Road Trip"
   B. "A trippin' road Trip"

10. A. *Teaching to Transgress*
    B. *Teaching To Transgress*

Part III

STRUCTURE AND STYLE OF SENTENCES AND PARAGRAPHS

Topics Covered in This Unit

1. Word Choice
2. Sentence Structure and Variety
3. Paragraph Structure

17

INTRODUCTION TO SENTENCE STRUCTURE AND STYLE

Should I begin my paper with a verb, an adjective, or some other part of speech altogether? How will this decision affect my reader and the delivery of my main idea? What's the danger in creating sentences that are all the same length or that begin with the same part of speech? What does my reader expect to see in a topic sentence and paragraph conclusion?

Contemplating such questions about structure and style and learning techniques for revising for structure and style will help you to write with more clarity, imagination, and unity. Learning how to analyze structure will enable you to improve your writing and reading comprehension, assisting you as both writer and critic of writing. Since readers expect your writing to perform certain functions in particular parts of a composition, it's crucial that you learn how to write effective sentences in those parts of compositions so that readers understand your ideas. For example, readers expect opening sentences to be attention-grabbing, topic sentences to introduce paragraph main ideas, and transitions to convey relationships between one area of a composition and another.

Well-structured sentences, paragraphs, and compositions achieve a distinctive degree of structural beauty, helping a composition to stand out for aesthetic as well as rhetorical reasons.

In this section, you'll learn techniques for analyzing and incorporating fundamental structural techniques, more of the anatomy (parts) and physiology (functions) of sentences and paragraphs.

> **TIP**
>
> Verbs are the most important part of speech. Try to organize your sentences around the most precise and stylish verb you can find.

Seven Tips for Writing Stylish Sentences

1. **Be concise**. Shakespeare and Pope tell us that "brevity is the soul of wit." Therefore you should say what you need to say in as *few words as possible*. Readers don't want to read extra words, and writers who can't identify the extraneous won't be creative or clear. Whenever possible, eliminate the verb *to be* from your sentences and avoid the verb *to be* before verbs (was driving, is believing).

2. **Be precise**. Say what you need to say accurately. In his essay "Fenimore Cooper's Literary Offences," Mark Twain enjoins us to use "the right word, not its second cousin." There's a difference between *happiness* and *elation*, *pain* and *anguish*. Use your resources to find the word that most precisely expresses your ideas.

3. **Diversify**. We've all had those monotone professors and teachers. They bore us because they don't mix it up. Vary the words you use, the way you begin and end a sentence or paragraph, the length of sentences and paragraphs, and whatever else you can do to inject the energy of diversity into your writing and hold your reader's interest.

4. **Tone up**. Is your piece going to use a tone that is sarcastic, intellectual, objective, bawdy, something else, or a mixture thereof? The right tone, and sometimes even the wrong tone, can be very effective.

5. **Know Thy Audience!** Choose a style that will help you to reach your audience. In formal academic writing, for example, it's advisable to resist the urge to use text message writing. Please don't substitute a *u* for *you*, an *idk* for *I don't know*, and, in general, avoid incorporating text message writing into your compositions. You should get to know your professor's tendencies and preferences.

6. **Question What You've Been Taught About Taboo Stylistic Choices**. Some professors and composition experts believe that it's bad form to use "I" in an essay or research paper. Students also tell me that they've been trained never to refer to their essay or parts of their essay. To those proscriptions, I say boo! Hiss! Consider the following example from Joseph Ellis, a historian who earned the Pulitzer prize for his writing ability. In one paragraph of his insightful book on our first president, *His Excellency, George Washington*, he violates both of these taboos several times. I've bolded

STRUCTURE AND STYLE OF SENTENCES AND PARAGRAPHS

those transgressions (which would have earned him the red ink of his composition instructors), hoping that you will follow in his footsteps and rebel against these silly stylistic rules.

> **I** began my odyssey with a question that had formed in **my** mind on the basis of earlier research in the papers of the revolutionary generation. It seemed that Benjamin Franklin was wiser than Washington. Alexander Hamilton was more brilliant, John Adams was better read, Thomas Jefferson was more intellectually sophisticated, James Madison was more politically astute. Yet each and all of these prominent figures acknowledged that Washington was their unquestioned superior…why was that? **In the pages that follow**, **I** have looked for an answer which lies buried within the folds of the most ambitious, determined, and potent personality of an age not lacking for worthy rivals. How he became that way, and what he then did with it, is **the story I try to tell**.

7. **Sentence Symmetry**. One part of a sentence should resonate with another part. One sentence should be symmetrical with another. This holds true for sentences in the same paragraph, different paragraphs, and in different parts of a composition, especially sentences that appear in conspicuous places such as opening sentences, topic sentences, and concluding sentences. So when you're trying to figure out how to build a sentence, or how to start the next sentence, or how to link one sentence back to a much earlier sentence, recycle the language and structure of those earlier sentences.

Two primary ways to create symmetry are by using a **parallel** (one part of a sentence is just like another) or a **contrast** (one part is the opposite of another).

Consider the following sentence from *Gulliver's Travels*, which is unified around several "sight" words in bold, and how this unity builds a key theme in the book about judging on appearances:

> "When I found myself on my feet, I **looked** about me, and must confess I never **beheld** a more entertaining **prospect**."

What We Can Learn about Sentence and Paragraph Style From Dr. Martin Luther King Jr.'s "I Have a Dream" speech

Remembered as a master orator who could deliver speeches that changed the world, Martin Luther King should also be appreciated for his beautiful prose. The exercise below introduces the main concepts of this unit by asking you to analyze some of the techniques of sentence and paragraph style in King's "I Have a Dream" speech. By understanding and applying the techniques he uses, you will be able to transform the style and structure of your sentences and paragraphs. Almost everything you need to learn about techniques for creating effective sentences and paragraphs appears in the first two paragraphs of this speech, which is a model for its cohesion, development, transitions, organization, and language.

Exercise 3.1a
Introduction to Sentence and Paragraph Style

Directions: Read the first two paragraphs of the speech. Then answer the questions on them.

> Five score years ago, a great American, in whose symbolic shadow we stand today, signed the Emancipation Proclamation. This momentous decree came as a great beacon light of hope to millions of Negro slaves who had been seared in the flames of withering injustice. It came as a joyous daybreak to end the long night of their captivity.
>
> But one hundred years later, the Negro still is not free. One hundred years later, the life of the Negro is still sadly crippled by the manacles of segregation and the chains of discrimination. One hundred years later, the Negro lives on a lonely island of poverty in the midst of a vast ocean of material prosperity. One hundred years later, the Negro is still languished in the corners of American society and finds himself an exile in his own land. And so we've come here today to dramatize a shameful condition.

1. Effective sentences and paragraphs use the **thesaurus approach** to convey and unify their ideas. That is, they are unified around a common idea (pain, for example) or technique (metaphor, contrast, literary reference, etc.). Let the language you use in one sentence, resonate with the language you use in other sentences, either by comparison or contrast so that your sentences are clearer, more organized and unified, and more stylish.

A. Which words in the <u>first paragraph</u> would you find in a thesaurus under the entry "light" and thereby link the sentences and unify the paragraph?

_____

_____

_____

B. Which words in the <u>first paragraph</u> would you find in a thesaurus under the entry for "dark" and thereby link the sentences and unify the paragraph?

_____

_____

_____

C. In the second sentence of the first paragraph, King uses the word "seared." With which other word in that sentence does "seared" resonate? What do the two words have in common?

_____

_____

_____

D. Which words in the <u>first two paragraphs</u> have associations with the concept of "time" and thereby link the sentences and unify the paragraph?

_____

_____

_____

   E. Which words in the <u>second paragraph</u> are metaphors or symbols that show alienation and thereby link the sentences and unify the paragraph?

_____

_____

_____

2. Effective paragraphs use **transitional sentences**, especially at the end and beginning, in order to establish relationships between ideas. A particularly stylish way to transition is to *avoid* using transitional words (e.g. however, in addition) between paragraphs and to instead let words at the end of one paragraph resonate with (either through comparison or contrast) words at the beginning of the next paragraph.

   A. Which words/ideas in the last sentence of the <u>first paragraph</u> relate to the words/phrases in the first sentence of the <u>second paragraph</u>, creating a smooth and logical link between the paragraphs?

_____

_____

_____

   B. An effective way to emphasize key points is through the technique of repetition. What phrase does the <u>second paragraph</u> repeat?

_____

_____

_____

C. What idea does that repetition emphasize?

_____

_____

_____

3. Good writers find the right words, choosing verbs, nouns, adjectives, and adverbs that best capture the ideas they want to convey.

   A. Which **verbs** does King use in the <u>2nd paragraph</u> to capture the "life of the Negro?" What do these verbs suggest about that life?

   _____

   _____

   _____

   B. Which **adjectives and nouns** does King use in the <u>second paragraph</u> in order to present clear images of the "life of the Negro?" What do these words suggest about that life?

   _____

   _____

   _____

   C. **Contrast** is a fundamental technique in writing that helps to illuminate each concept contrasted so that the reader more clearly understands each idea. What are some of the contrasts you see throughout the <u>first two paragraphs</u>? Consider contrasts in adjacent sentences and even within sentences.

_____

_____

_____

* Write two paragraphs using the ingredients King uses. While you could write your own I-have-a-dream speech, feel free to write about anything you'd like as long as you incorporate at least three of the approaches presented in questions 1–3. Label your sentences and paragraphs to indicate where you've used, for example, the thesaurus approach, effective verbs, or a stylish transition.

_____

_____

_____

_____

_____

_____

_____

_____

_____

_____

_____

18

CHOOSING THE RIGHT WORD

In "Politics and the English Language," George Orwell argues that cliché words and phrases produce a lack of clarity and encourage slovenly thinking. In fact, failure to choose an original word, for Orwell, shows that a writer isn't a free thinker—that the writer is a lazy, conforming follower.

The best way to avoid the error of using an imprecise or unclear word or phrase is to break out the **dictionary** and **thesaurus**. By using these reference books, you'll not only find the right word, but also you'll improve your vocabulary and strengthen your ability to think and communicate clearly and independently. One more advantage of using the dictionary and thesaurus is that you will be able to create unity of language and precision of tone and mood. If your composition is about betrayal, you should incorporate several words that are synonyms for *betrayal*. This use of diversified repetition of language will unify your writing around key ideas, helping you to communicate your points clearly and creatively. The writing will be more beautiful and more coherent as a result.

Words of the Conformist Writer

Here is a list of a few conspicuous words that tend to be imprecise, and that should, generally, be avoided. Yes, they're accessible, but they are usually the first words you think of, not necessarily the right words.

Good	Bad	Nice
Thing	Sad	Happy

Exercise 3.2a Precision and Word Choice

<u>Directions:</u> Circle the thesaurus word that transforms the imprecise italicized word to a more precise and specific word that captures the main idea of the sentence and resonates with other parts of the sentence.

1. I feel *bad* because I missed the winning shot.

    Thesaurus: unhappy, evil, malicious, poor, frustrated

2. He is a *good* professor who knows his material very well.

    Thesaurus: nice, competent, moral, pleasing

3. My friend is so *nice* that even strangers feel comfortable talking to her.

    Thesaurus: amiable, lovely, okay, pleasurable

4. That house has *a nice* dining room.

Thesaurus: an exceptional, a great, an elegant, an excellent

5. I felt so *bad* that I had to ask my boss if I could end my shift early so that I could go home and feel better.

    Thesaurus: nauseated, malevolent, depraved, nefarious

6. The *sad* girl didn't eat for three days when her sister died.

    Thesaurus: unhappy, emo, anguished, poor

7. The quarterback's throws are very *good*.

    Thesaurus: generous, excellent, accurate, benevolent

8. Since my girlfriend broke up with me, I've felt *sad and lonely*.

    Thesaurus: disappointed, upset, forlorn, pessimistic

    > **Is a Thesaurus Sufficient?**
    >
    > Remember that a thesaurus isn't enough. The thesaurus offers synonyms. Sometimes those synonyms are distant cousins of the word you need, so you must use the dictionary as well to confirm that the word you have chosen is in the immediate family of the word you need. As Mark Twain said, choosing the right word is like knowing the difference between lightning and the lightning bug, so use a dictionary!

9. I was so *happy* when I won the $10 million Lotto jackpot.

    Thesaurus: convivial, intoxicated, ecstatic, mirthful

10. I feel *happy* for those great times we shared all those years ago.

Thesaurus: lugubrious, nostalgic, merry, emotional

Exercise 3.2b   Precision and Word Choice

<u>Directions</u>: The following sentences require revision for word choice because the underlined sections do *not* convey the right tone or mood. Read the italicized explanation of what the writer wants to convey in order to choose the best answer.

1. After his mother told him that he can't have a cookie until after dinner, little Jimmie <u>walked</u> up the stairs and <u>closed </u>his bedroom door.

The writer wants to convey that the character is <u>frustrated and bratty</u>: which verb pair most accurately conveys that idea?

    A. ran…shut
    B. ambled…slammed
    C. stomped…slammed

2. We rowed across the pond in silence, our paddles gently <u>hitting</u> the tranquil surface of the water.

The writer wants to establish a mood of <u>peace and harmony</u>: which choice most accurately conveys that idea?

    A. striking
    B. brushing
    C. swatting

3. "Don't ever hit your brother," his father <u>said</u>.

The writer wants to establish the father's <u>indignation</u>*: which choice most accurately conveys that idea?*

    A. announced
    B. growled
    C. uttered

4. As I lay tanning on the blanket, I inhaled the salty air and enjoyed the background <u>noise</u> of the waves <u>slamming</u> ashore.

The writer wants to use some of the five senses to capture the pleasant aspects of the beach: which choice most accurately conveys that idea?

    A. music…washing
    B. clamor…banging
    C. reverberations…crashing

5. After making the winning shot, Johnson <u>moved</u> triumphantly across the court.

Which choice best captures how a very pleased person would act in the situation?

    A. strutted
    B. walked
    C. paced

6. My younger sister <u>asked</u> me not to text while driving.

Which is the best word for this situation?

    A. ordered
    B. beseeched
    C. commanded

7. General Prescott <u>told</u> the troops to take no prisoners.

Which is the best word for this situation?

    A. begged
    B. invited
    C. ordered

8. Clumsy Schecter <u>fell</u> on the ice and bruised her knee.

Which is the best word for this situation?

    A. slipped
    B. landed
    C. descended

9. The <u>ugly</u> bookcase hasn't been cleaned in several months.

Which is the best word for this situation?

    A. ancient
    B. old
    C. dusty

10. Willi's <u>dumb</u> thesis didn't have enough support to persuade me to change my opinion.

Which is the best word for this situation?

A. ignorant
B. unsubstantiated
C. vapid

19

CONCISION

In his "Essay on Criticism," Alexander Pope wrote that words are like leaves in that "where they most abound,/ Much fruit of sense beneath is rarely found." Therefore, it's advisable to use as few words as possible to convey your ideas. Don't use the fanciest expression; use the one that makes most sense. Don't say what you need to say in many words; say it in as few words as possible. Too many words make for too much reading. The longer the composition, the less likely it is that readers will read it. The wordier your writing is, the more likely it is to create confusion.

Sometimes the solution to wordiness is **deleting unnecessary words**; other times, it's advisable to **substitute a one-word synonym** for a wordy expression; still another way to produce concision is by **combining sentences**. In this section, you'll practice using each of those solutions to wordiness.

Exercise 3.3a   Concision

<u>Directions (1–5):</u> Delete redundant and unnecessary language so that sentences are clear and concise. Write the revised sentence on the lines below.

Example: ~~Every year,~~ annually, my uncle takes me to a Knicks game.

Revised: <u>My uncle takes me to a Knicks game annually.</u>

1. Every winter when it's cold, we travel to Great Wolf Lodge for indoor swimming.

    _____

    _____

    _____

    _____

2. In today's world, people currently borrow too much and save too little.

    _____

    _____

    _____

    _____

3. The students collaborated together on the task.

    _____

    _____

_____

_____

4. Because you didn't study is the reason you failed.

_____

_____

_____

_____

5. There is a consensus of opinion about wordiness: avoid it!

_____

_____

_____

_____

Exercise 3.3b   More Concision

Directions (1–5): Condense the following sentences by deleting unnecessary words and finding one-word synonyms for wordy expressions. Then rewrite the sentences on the lines below.

Example: There are five cars parked outside the house in the driveway.

Revised: Five cars are parked in the driveway.

1. On the chance that you forget to call, don't worry, I'll call you.

   _____

   _____

   _____

   _____

2. The fact that A-Rod used steroids and didn't tell the truth about it should prevent him from entering the Hall of Fame.

   _____

   _____

   _____

   _____

3. As one might have predicted, the New York Jets disappointed their fans.

   _____

   _____

   _____

   _____

4. Being that you're a nice person, I would like to ask you to the prom.

   _____

   _____

_____

_____

5. They are giving me a hard time and annoying me every day.

_____

_____

_____

_____

Exercise 3.3c   Concision through Combining

<u>Directions (1–5)</u>: Choose the answer that most concisely combines the wordy sentences.

1. My house is large. It's over six thousand square feet. Since it's so large, it has more than enough room for guests who want to visit.

   A. Since my house is over six thousand square feet, it has ample space for guests who enjoy visiting.
   B. Since my house is over six thousand square feet, it has ample space for guests.
   C. Since my house is so large, containing more than six thousand square feet, it has lots of room for guests who want to visit.

2. Shakespeare is the best poet ever to have written. His plays are more interesting than any other writer's plays. In addition, his ideas have stood the test of time,

enduring for hundreds of years, which is the reason why he is the greatest of all writers.

A. Shakespeare is the greatest poet and playwright, and since his ideas have stood the test of time, he is the greatest writer of all.

B. Shakespeare's poetry is the best, his plays are the most interesting, and the ideas that he writers about have lasted a long time, so he is the writer who is better than all other writers.

C. The greatest poet to have produced poetry and playwright to have written plays, Shakespeare is also the writer whose writings have endured, which is why he is the greatest writer of all.

3. At 1 p.m. in the afternoon, I ate the lunch that was made. I ate dinner at 7 p.m. in the evening. I didn't dine on dessert at all.

A. I ate lunch at 1 p.m. and dinner at 7 p.m., but I didn't eat dessert at all.

B. I ate my lunch at 1 p.m. and ate my dinner at 7 p.m., but I didn't dine on dessert at all in the a.m. or p.m.

C. I ate the food that was made for lunch at 1 p.m., and I ate the dinner that was made at 7 p.m., but I didn't have the dessert that was made at all that day.

4. Despite the fact that he studied, he still didn't earn a score that he found to be satisfactory. He was disappointed.

A. Despite the fact that he studied, he earned a disappointing grade that wasn't as high as he had hoped. As a result, he was dissatisfied.
B. Although he studied, he didn't earn a satisfactory grade.
C. Although he studied, he failed to achieve a gratifying score that pleased him.

5. Talented at throwing, hitting, running, and fielding, she's an amazing softball player. She excels in all those areas, which is the reason why colleges want to recruit her.

A. Because she's talented in all areas of softball, colleges seek to recruit her.
B. The fact that she's talented in all areas of the game of softball is the reason why colleges want to recruit her.
C. Colleges want to recruit her because of her talents in hitting, running, throwing, and fielding. Her excellence in all areas makes her a great player.

20

SENTENCE STYLE AND VARIETY

What happens when you listen to a speaker who never varies his tone or sentence length? You get bored, just as Ferris Buehler's classmates were bored by their economics teacher's monotone voice. And what happens when speakers emphasize the wrong words? You get confused, as Austin Power's audience was when he put the emphasis on the wrong syllable after being awakened from a cryogenic freeze. When you revise, think about ways to vary the structure and length of your sentences so that you can properly emphasize key ideas and maintain your reader's interest. Since sentence variety helps to **clarify relationships** between ideas and to **maintain the reader's interest**, consider using non-conventional ways to express your thoughts.

The conventional sentence in English is structured with the subject first and then the verb.

Example: Puppies are cute. [*Puppies* is the subject; *are* is the verb.]

This subject-first sentence structure is perfectly suitable, but if it's the only way you structure your sentences, you'll bore your readers and miss opportunities to emphasize more important ideas.

Since first and last words are the key places for emphasis in a sentence, think about **opening your sentences** with a different part of speech, especially verbs, adverbs, adjectives, and prepositions.

Sentence flow

One sentence should clearly relate to its neighbors, funneling down the paragraph in a logical and fluid manner. Try using the thesaurus approach to sentence creation. Consider building a sentence around a synonym for a word that appears in the sentence that you've already written.

If you want to emphasize action, place a form of the **verb first**.

Example: Chasing puppies is fun.

If you want to emphasize the nature of the action, **begin with an adverb**.

Example: Loudly barking dogs annoy me.

If you want to emphasize a descriptive element, put the **adjective first**.

Example: Fluffy puppies feel soft.

If you want to emphasize location or orientation, place the **preposition first**.

Example: Underneath the dog's collar you'll see a tick.

The parts of speech above will help you with variety of openings, and they'll also help you to **combine for variety of length**. There are many other ways to combine for variety of length, especially by **combining sentences**. Consider the following methods for varying the length of your sentences.

1. Vary length by combining sentences with a **subordinating conjunction**

after, although, because, since, while, etc.

2. Vary length and openings by combining sentences with a relative pronoun

who, whom, whoever, whomever, whose, which, that

3. Vary length and openings by combining sentences with a **coordinating conjunction** (FANBOYS)

for, and, nor, but, or, yet, so

4. Vary length and openings by combining sentences with a **semicolon + conjunctive adverb + comma**

; consequently, ; however, ; instead, ; therefore,

Exercise 3.4a   Varying Sentence Openings

Directions: In the following questions, use forms of the verb, adverbs, adjectives, and prepositional phrases at the beginning of sentences. Follow the directions to achieve variety of opening and length. Remember to avoid modifier

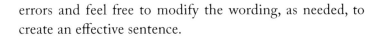
errors and feel free to modify the wording, as needed, to create an effective sentence.

Example: I failed my midterm. I disappointed my parents, my professor, and myself. [Begin with the verb *failing* and combine the two sentences to add variety of opening and length]

Revised: <u>Failing my midterm, I disappointed my parents, my professor, and myself.</u>

1. He sped down the street. He lost control of his car. [Begin with the verb *speeding* (participle) and combine the two sentences to add variety of opening and length]

   _____

   _____

   _____

   _____

2. We have changed our opinion on the matter. We now believe that you are right. [Begin with the verb *changing* (participle) and combine the two sentences to add variety of opening and length]

   _____

   _____

   _____

   _____

3. I foolishly disregarded my professor's suggestions. I ended up failing the exam and the course. [Begin with the adverb *foolishly* and combine the two sentences to add variety of opening and length]

_____

_____

_____

_____

4. The thug brutally smashed the victim's skull. He was a man of no conscience. [Begin with the adverb and combine the two sentences to add variety of opening and length]

> **Avoid modifier errors**
>
> Remember to avoid modifier errors when combining sentences. See section 2.6 for modifier errors.

_____

_____

_____

_____

5. There is gum stuck underneath the desk. It is white and dry. [Begin with the prepositional phrase *underneath the desk* and combine the two sentences to add variety of opening and length]

_____

_____

_____

_____

6. An eerie old elm tree lurks in my back yard. It spooks my little brother. [Begin with the prepositional phrase *in my back yard* and combine the two sentences to add variety of opening and length]

----

7. The motel is dingy. It smells putrid. [Begin with the article and adjective *The dingy* and combine the two sentences to add variety of opening and length]

----

8. This bedroom is a filthy pigsty. The bedroom needs to be cleaned. [Begin with the article and adjective *A filthy* and combine the two sentences to add variety of opening and length]

----

9. He drove so slowly down the street in his hybrid vehicle. He was even passed by kids on tricycles. [Begin

with the verb *Driving* and combine the two sentences to add variety of opening and length]

_____

_____

_____

_____

10. We were knock-kneed and coughing like hags. We cursed as we marched through the sludge. [Adapted from Wilfred Owen.] [Begin with the adjective *Knock-kneed* and combine the two sentences to add variety of opening and length]

_____

_____

_____

_____

Exercise 3.4b Variety via Coordinating Conjunctions

<u>Directions</u>: In the following questions, combine sentences with coordinating conjunctions in order to add variety of length and correctly capture the relationship between the two sentences. Choose the answer that most effectively combines the sentences.

1. In most cases, gestation occurs inside females. In the case of seahorses, males are the ones who give birth.

A. In most cases, gestation occurs inside females, and in the case of seahorses, males are the ones who give birth.

B. In most cases, gestation occurs inside females, so in the case of seahorses, males are the ones who give birth.

C. In most cases, gestation occurs inside females, but in the case of seahorses, males are the ones who give birth.

2. During courtship, the genitals of the male honeybee explode inside the queen. They break off inside her body.

A. During courtship, the genitals of the male honeybee explode inside the queen, yet they break off inside her body.

B. During courtship, the genitals of the male honeybee explode inside the queen, and they break off inside her body.

C. During courtship, the genitals of the male honeybee explode inside the queen, but they break off inside her body.

Coordinating Conjunctions

Remember FANBOYS when thinking about coordinating conjunctions: *for, and, nor, but, or, yet, so.*

3. During courtship, male anglerfish bite into females. They must hold onto each other in order to reproduce.

A. During courtship, male anglerfish bite into females, for they must hold onto each other in order to reproduce.

B. During courtship, male anglerfish bite into females, but they must hold onto each other in order to reproduce.

C. During courtship, male anglerfish bite into females, nor do they hold onto each other until death.

4. Some plants have learned to mimic the pheromones of butterflies. Plants haven't learned to mimic flight.

A. Some plants have learned to mimic the pheromones of butterflies, yet plants haven't learned to mimic flight.

B. Some plants have learned to mimic the pheromones of butterflies, or plants haven't learned to mimic flight.

C. Some plants have learned to mimic the pheromones of butterflies because plants haven't learned to mimic flight.

5. The creature was a reptile. I knew it would have scaly skin and be warm-blooded.

A. The creature was a reptile, but I knew it would have scaly skin and be warm blooded.

B. The creature was a reptile, so I knew it would have scaly skin and be warm blooded.

C. The creature was a reptile, yet I knew it would have scaly skin and be warm blooded.

6. The snake is likely dying. The reason may be that it has internal parasites or that you overfed it.

A. The snake is likely dying, and the reason may be that it has internal parasites or that you overfed it.

    B. The snake is likely dying, yet the reason may be that it has internal parasites or that you overfed it.

    C. The snake is likely dying, but the reason may be that it has internal parasites or that you overfed it.

7. Crepuscular animals are active at dusk. I come right before sunset with my camera to photograph them.

    A. Crepuscular animals are active at dusk, for I come right before sunset with my camera to photograph them.

    B. Crepuscular animals are active at dusk, so I come right before sunset with my camera to photograph them.

    C. Crepuscular animals are active at dusk, nor do I come right before sunset with my camera to photograph them.

8. Some painted turtles survive harsh winters without breathing. They have developed the ability to exchange oxygen and carbon dioxide through their skin.

    A. Painted turtles survive harsh winters without breathing, but they have developed the ability to exchange oxygen and carbon dioxide through their skin.

    B. Painted turtles survive harsh winters without breathing, so they have developed the ability to exchange oxygen and carbon dioxide through their skin.

    C. Painted turtles survive harsh winters without breathing, for they have developed the ability to exchange oxygen and carbon dioxide through their skin.

9. Hatchling Alligator Snapping turtles are cute. Hatchling
    Mississippi Map turtles are cuter.

    A. The Hatchling Alligator Snapping turtles are cute,
       and hatchling Mississippi Map turtles are cuter.
    B. The Hatchling Alligator Snapping turtles are cute,
       so hatchling Mississippi Map turtles are cuter.
    C. The Hatchling Alligator Snapping turtles are cute,
       but hatchling Mississippi Map turtles are cuter.

10. Researchers don't know whether the great white shark
    was eaten by an enormous cannibal shark, or some
    other massive sea creature. They do know that whatever
    ate the great white has an internal body temperature of
    seventy degrees Fahrenheit.

    A. Researchers don't know whether the great white
       shark was eaten by an enormous cannibal shark, or
       some other massive sea creature, and they do know
       that whatever ate the great white has an internal
       body temperature of seventy degrees Fahrenheit.
    B. Researchers don't know whether the great white
       shark was eaten by an enormous cannibal shark, or
       some other massive sea creature, but they do know
       that whatever ate the great white has an internal
       body temperature of seventy degrees Fahrenheit.
    C. Researchers don't know whether the great white
       shark was eaten by an enormous cannibal shark, or
       some other massive sea creature, for they do know
       that whatever ate the great white has an internal
       body temperature of seventy degrees Fahrenheit.

Exercise 3.4c   Variety via Subordinating Conjunctions

<u>Directions</u>: Combine the sentences by choosing from the word bank a subordinating conjunction that correctly expresses the relationship between the two sentences. Feel free to modify the wording as needed in order to create an effective sentence.

Example: You didn't come to Sunday dinner. Mom was disappointed.

Revised: Because you didn't come to Sunday dinner, Mom was disappointed.

Common Subordinating Conjunctions

after	in order	that
although	now that	though
as	once	unless
because	rather than	when
before	since	whereas
even though	so that	while
if	than	

1. I sprinted the entire way home. I passed out from exhaustion.

_____

_____

_____

_____

2. Kitty Genovese pleaded for help. Some bystanders did nothing to help her.

_____

_____

_____

_____

3. Our pitcher gave up only one earned run. We still lost the game.

_____

_____

_____

_____

4. You didn't show any gratitude. They think you're rude.

_____

_____

_____

_____

5. Rick began racing competitively five years ago. He has won several medals.

_____

_____

_____

_____

6. My mother cleans the dishes. I wipe the countertops.

_____

_____

_____

_____

7. We ate dinner. Then we had dessert.

_____

_____

_____

_____

8. You are funny and rich. I don't want to marry you.

_____

_____

_____

_____

9. My mother and father never saved a cent. They never had money for emergencies.

_____

_____

_____

_____

10. I love you very much. I don't love the way your breath smells at this moment.

_____

_____

_____

_____

Exercise 3.4d Variety via Conjunctive Adverbs

<u>Directions</u>: Combine the sentences by choosing a conjunctive adverb that correctly expresses the relationship between the two sentences.

Example: I didn't study very much or attend class. I failed.

Revised: I didn't study very much or attend class; consequently, I failed.

In these exercises, use only the following conjunctive adverbs: *consequently, however, instead, therefore*

1. I should have stayed up late and finished my paper. I watched Monday night football, gorged on hot wings, and procrastinated on my Calculus homework.

_____

_____

_____

_____

2. You lied, you cheated, and you never said you're sorry. You no longer have a girlfriend.

Conjunctive Adverbs

A more complete list of **conjunctive adverbs** includes the following: *accordingly, furthermore, moreover, similarly, also, hence, namely, still, anyway, however, nevertheless, then, besides, incidentally, thereafter, certainly, indeed, nonetheless, therefore, consequently, instead, now, thus, likewise, otherwise, undoubtedly, and meanwhile.*

3. On Thursdays, I usually study before going to the gym. Today, I went to Friendly's and skipped the gym.

4. For a year, I put ten dollars per paycheck into my savings. I still don't have enough money for hair transplants.

5. Jennifer showed up for class, submitted her work on time, and asked for help. She earned an A.

6. Richard attended every lecture, completed his work on time, and asked for help. He earned only a C+.

_____

_____

_____

_____

7. Although he is friendly, Dr. Jones is an incompetent professor. His students don't learn much from him.

_____

_____

_____

_____

8. Superintendents are highly paid and wield a lot of power. They must show personal and financial restraint.

_____

_____

_____

_____

9. Most students buy their textbooks online. I buy them directly from the bookstore.

_____

_____

_____

10. If you come too close, you may get burned. If you stay too far away, you may not be warmed by the heat.

_____

_____

_____

_____

Exercise 3.4e   Variety via Relative Pronouns

<u>Directions</u>: Combine the sentences by using the relative pronoun requested in brackets. Feel free to modify the wording as needed in order to achieve sentence variety.

Example: The novel was interesting. I read it in one day. [Combine using *that*]

Revised: The novel was so interesting that I read it in one day.

Relative Pronouns

Relative pronouns introduce clauses that modify main clauses. That is, they provide more information about the main clause. Relative pronouns include the following: *who, whom, whoever, whomever, whose, which,* and *that.*

1. The store sells everything you need. It is not far from here. [Combine using *which*]

_____

_____

_____

2. The writer didn't revise for grammar. He usually proofreads carefully. [Combine using *who*]

   _____

   _____

   _____

   _____

3. Citi Field has a capacity of forty-five thousand people.
   It opened in 2009. [Combine using *which*]

   _____

   _____

   _____

   _____

4. The man perished in a fire. His son is a fireman. [Combine
   using *whose*]

   _____

   _____

   _____

   _____

5. Jennifer was exhausted and ill. She showed up anyway,
   and performed beautifully. [Combine using *who*]

   _____

   _____

   _____

6. Michael is a versatile musician. His mother was a talented guitarist. [Combine using *whose*]

7. I bought her a puppy. She is the woman I love. [Combine using *whom*]

8. I can't find the book. You lent it to me yesterday. [Combine using *that*]

9. We waited more than an hour for the advisor. He was stuck in traffic on the Long Island Expressway. [Combine using *who*]

---

10. Last summer we vacationed in Nice. Nice is located in southern France on the Mediterranean Sea. [Combine using *which*]

21

ACTIVE AND PASSIVE VOICE

Active voice and passive voice are terms that describe connections between the way a verb and subject act. In an <u>active voice</u> sentence, the subject does the action.

Example: Goring passes the puck to Bossy. [subj=*Goring* who is active, he *passes*]

In a <u>passive voice</u> sentence, the subject receives the action, or is acted upon. It's passive.

Example: The puck was passed by Goring to Bossy. [subj=*puck*, which is passive, it gets *passed* by Goring]

The presence of the verb *to be* before the past participle usually indicates that a sentence is written in passive voice.

Past Participle

Participles are forms of the verb. Regular verbs form the past participle by adding -ed, -d, -t, -en, or -n to verbs preceded by tho vorb *to be*. Example: The paper was chewed. Irregular verbs often use the verb to be before verbs that end in –n. Example: I was driven to the store.

Example: This sentence is written in passive voice. [Note how the verb to be (is) precedes the past participle (written)]

What are the virtues of active voice? Active voice tends to require **fewer words** than passive voice, often is **clearer**, and usually invites the use of more effective verbs. Although it's usually advisable to choose active voice, there are occasions in which passive voice more effectively meets the expectations of an audience and more accurately emphasizes the relationships between subject and verb.

When is it <u>acceptable to use passive voice</u>? Bearing in mind that there is nothing grammatically incorrect about passive voice, recognize the following situations and purposes of passive voice:

1. **Scientific writing**, such as lab reports. Consider this example: *The liquid was observed boiling at 180 degrees Fahrenheit.* Although an active voiced sentence more clearly and concisely expresses an idea, the science field often prefers passive voice, despite, or perhaps because of, its failure to clearly identify the subject. Just who was it who observed the liquid to boil at 180 degrees? In science, it doesn't seem to matter, because science cares more about the experiment than it does about the experimenter. Or at least it wants us to think so!

2. **To emphasize** or **de-emphasize**. If you don't know who performed an action, or if you want to shift the emphasis, use passive voice. Consider the following sentence: *The dirty clothes were left on the bedroom floor.* This sentence might be more effective as it is in passive

voice because its author might not know who left the clothes on the floor.

3. When you want to **conceal the identity** of the figure responsible for the action. Consider this example that we hear from deceitful politicians who want us to think they're taking responsibility: *Bad judgment was shown, errors were made, and lives were lost.*

   In general, for reasons of clarity and concision, it's advisable to **write in active voice**.

Exercise 3.5a   Identifying Active and Passive Voice

Directions: Identify whether the sentences are in active or passive voice.

Example: Mick Taylor played a melodic solo. Active

1. Jonah ran away from the Lord. _____

2. The train arrived five minutes late. _____

3. Customers were insulted. _____

4. The wedding ring was left on the mistress's nightstand. _____

5. Four milliliters of sodium chloride were pipetted into an Erlenmeyer flask. _____

Exercise 3.5b   Voice in Context

Directions: Revise the sentence so that it is consistent with the voice indicated in parentheses. Bonus points if you can explain how the conversions affect emphasis and readers' understanding.

Example: I lied. I hurt people. I made costly mistakes. (Convert to *passive voice*)

Revised: Lies were told, people were hurt, and costly mistakes were made.

1. I spilled the milk on the table. (Convert to passive)

_____

_____

_____

2. Oswald assassinated Kennedy. (Convert to passive)

_____

_____

_____

3. The scene was filmed in black and white. (Convert to active)

_____

_____

_____

4. The bill was signed by the president. (Convert to active)

_____

_____

_____

5. The suspect was seen fleeing from the scene of the crime by witnesses. (Convert to active)

_____

_____

_____

Exercise 3.5c   More Voice

Directions: Decide whether the active or passive voice version of the sentence is more effective for each scenario. Then provide a rationale for your decision. Try to base that rationale on the scenario and the information at the beginning of this section on voice.

1. Scenario: You're a congressman who had an extramarital affair, and you're trying to write a sentence for a press conference about the scandal. You don't want to admit to any wrongdoing, but you do want to acknowledge the affair. Which sentence would you use?

    A. It's regrettable that the mistakes that were made have impacted my family and my constituency.
    B. I'm sorry that my unethical conduct eroded the trust of my family and constituency.

Rationale:

_____

_____

_____

_____

2. Scenario: You're writing a lab report for biology and your instructor told you to de-emphasize your role in the experiment. Which sentence would you use?

    A. After I crossed forty wild-type male drosophila with forty mutant females, I determined the number of offspring of each type.
    B. After the forty wild-type male drosophila were crossed with forty mutant females, the number of offspring of each type was determined.

Rationale:

_____

_____

_____

_____

3. Scenario: Your parents are furious that they came home to a messy house. They want to know who's responsible, but you don't want to reveal the identify of the perpetrator. Which sentence would you use?

    A. John had a party here and he didn't clean up—it's his fault.

B. I'm sorry that a mess was made and that you're so upset.

Rationale:

_____

_____

_____

_____

4. Scenario: You're revising a paper for a creative writing course, deciding upon which sentence more effectively emphasizes Ursula's behavior. Which sentence would you choose?

   A. Ursula abandoned her child, dumping it at the door of the orphanage.
   B. The child was abandoned by its mother, who left it at the door of the orphanage.

Rationale:

_____

_____

_____

_____

5. Scenario: Your business writing professor has asked you to revise for concision and clarity. Which sentence would you choose?

A. The taxes were prepared by the accountant, and all of the receipts were filed by the secretary.
B. The accountant prepared the taxes, and the secretary filed the receipts.

Rationale:

_____

_____

_____

_____

22

EFFECTIVE PARAGRAPH STRUCTURE

Paragraphs are compositions in microcosm. They have introductions (topic sentences), bodies, and conclusions. Readers have certain expectations of sentences in each of these three parts. For example, they expect introductory sentences to preview and resonate with what the rest of the paragraph is about. In bodies, they hope to see examples that relate to the ideas in the topic sentences. In paragraph conclusions, readers anticipate that writers will summarize the main idea of the paragraph, discuss the meaning of ideas, and transition to the next paragraph. Paragraphs should be symmetrical, with topic sentences and paragraph conclusions mirroring each other, and bodies serving as places to support ideas. By creating this **unity of idea and structure**, paragraphs are more likely to communicate their main points and to do so in an aesthetically alluring manner.

There are a few key places where sentences need to be particularly effective in order for readers to understand your main points and appreciate the structure of your writing.

While there are many ways to structure a paragraph, and although topic sentences can be the first, middle, or last sentence of a paragraph, it's advisable to master the technique of structuring paragraphs with *topic sentences as the first sentence* for a few reasons. Namely, by placing the topic sentence first, writers will increase the chances that readers are prepared for what follows, and if readers are prepared for what follows, they are more likely to understand the main idea of the paragraph.

What does an effective **topic sentence** look like? An effective topic sentence is specific and very limited in scope. Topic sentences should *not* be stew (lots of ideas mixed together). A paragraph is a piece of beef or a potato, but not both mixed together into a stew. Make *one* point per paragraph in the topic sentence, and you'll increase the likelihood that you and your readers understand the main idea. Topic sentences should also <u>align with thesis/main idea</u> and paper guidelines. By their nature, topic sentences look backward and forward. The language of a topic sentence should resonate with the language of the end of the <u>previous</u> paragraph and the content of the <u>current</u> paragraph. They should resonate with the language of the assignment guidelines and connect to the title, thesis/main idea, and paper conclusion.

Bodies and conclusions are also two-faced. Bodies should build on the topic sentences that precede them. Conclusions should resonate with the language of the topic

> **Walk Before You Run**
>
> Although this approach to paragraphing may seems stiff and formulaic, these structural skills are necessary to possess before a writer employs more daring and original approaches. Go back to section 3.1 and see the exercise on Martin Luther King's "I Have a Dream" speech. King uses many of the structural techniques described on this page.

sentence of the paragraph in which conclusions appear and introduce the ideas coming in the next paragraph.

The following exercise is designed to teach you how to revise for paragraph unity. When you read your papers, do what you do here: read your topic sentences and paragraph bodies, and ask whether the bodies clearly build on, and relate to, topic sentences.

Exercise 3.6A Topic Sentences and Paragraph Unity

<u>Directions</u>: In the following exercise, you'll see three topic sentences for three different paragraphs. Each is followed by sentences that are supposed to support the topic sentences. Determine whether the following paragraphs are unified. Strike through any of the supporting sentences (A–F) that don't belong because they don't clearly relate to and build on the topic sentence.

Topic Sentence 1: In *The Empire Strikes Back*, Luke attains enlightenment.

A. Succumbing to the dark side, Darth Vader never learns about goodness and the force.
B. During his adventure, Luke acquires the wisdom that he needs to become a Jedi.
C. While battling evil, Luke learns a lot about himself and his destiny.
D. George Lucas, the director of the <u>Star Wars</u> saga, is a brilliant and innovative director.

E. His skill with the light saber, his ability to fly, and his belief in himself reveal that Luke is a wise figure.

F. C3PO and R2D2 are very intelligent companions of Luke Skywalker, and they add comic relief to the Star Wars saga.

Topic Sentence 2: In order to write a unified body paragraph, a writer should revise for the following:

A. Make sure the topic sentence previews or summarizes the paragraph's main idea.

B. Save your work often so that you don't lose important sentences you've written.

C. Create an interesting thesis and compelling title so that the reader is eager to read the paper.

D. Incorporate examples in the body of the paragraph, making sure that the examples relate to, and build upon, the topic sentence.

E. Develop the body paragraph by explaining the significance of those examples, especially focusing on the ways in which the examples support the topic sentence claims.

F. Create a paragraph conclusion that summarizes the paragraph's main idea and transitions to the next body paragraph.

Topic Sentence 3: Ted Williams is probably the greatest hitter of all time.

A. Williams, also known as "The Splendid Splinter," was a tremendous power hitter, belting over 500 home runs in his career.

B. In addition to power, Williams hit for average, garnering the fourth highest career batting average in Major League Baseball history.

C. Also known as "The Splendid Splinter," Williams is the last man to hit .400, batting an amazing .406 in 1941.

D. Ted Williams was also a manager of the Washington Senators and Texas Rangers, but he didn't excel in that capacity.

E. Having lost three years of his prime to service in World War II and two more years as a fighter pilot in the Korean War, Ted Williams's hitting statistics are even more spectacular than they appear since he would have achieved more had he served five years of his career to the military.

F. Some say Babe Ruth is even better than Ted Williams since "The Babe" was an all-time great hitter and pitcher while "The Splendid Splinter" never pitched.

Topic Sentence 4: Traveling isn't fun, but vacationing is.

A. I love traveling by train.

B. While vacationing in Ecuador five years ago, I was bitten by a venomous snake.

C. When I am in Charleston, I enjoy sunbathing, jet skiing, and having drinks on the rooftop bars while the sun sets.

D. Although I don't enjoy the twenty-hour car ride to Orlando, I do love playing at the amusement parks.

E. My mother's favorite destination is Istanbul, but she hasn't been there in almost thirty years.

F. I enjoy watching the view from the plane when I fly to Las Vegas, where I have a blast dancing, eating, and playing blackjack.

Revising Paragraphs for Organization

The following exercises will help you with organization and unity. As you revise paragraphs, make sure the information you provide is relevant. A sentence is relevant if it relates to its neighboring sentences and the main idea; if it doesn't relate to its neighbors and its main idea, consider rewording sentences so that they do fit, moving them to more relevant places, or cutting them entirely. In this exercise, you'll work on identifying irrelevant sentences that a writer would eventually have to (1) modify so that the sentences align with the topic sentence, (2) move to a more relevant place, or (3) cut.

Exercise 3.6b   Paragraph Unity

Directions: Read each paragraph for its main idea. Read it again and see which sentences interfere with the flow because they are irrelevant. Then ~~strike through~~ the sentences that do not fit next to their neighbors because they don't relate.

Paragraph 1:

¹My brother Steve is a good guy. ²He lives in a lovely, four-thousand-square-foot white house down the street. ³Steve always helps people in need. ⁴Whether it's the lady who can't change a flat or the man who needs help starting

the lawnmower, he's always there for people. [5]Some people in his neighborhood have lawns that are meticulously landscaped. [6]If you need to talk, you can call him anytime, and he'd give you his last cent so that you wouldn't have to do without. [7]I love him the way he is and hope that I can emulate his virtues. [8]His wife isn't very nice.

Paragraph 2:

[1]Although they're elusive, hatchling turtles can be found if you know where to look. [2]Eager to avoid predatory birds, hatchlings tend to hide on the underside of a pond's surface grasses and weeds. [3]Hatchlings are so tiny and cute, which is why people love them. [4]When not hiding right beneath the surface, hatchlings nestle in the mud at the bottom of ponds. [5]Turtles lay their eggs on land, so if you want to find a hatchling before it hatches, look for a buried nest close to water but on higher, drier ground. [6]Hatchlings are reptiles, which means they have scales and are cold blooded.

Paragraph 3:

[1]Eating out is expensive. [2]I'm the type of person who prefers to date people who listen and ask questions about what I've said. [3]Before you call me egotistical for wanting an attentive listener, you should know that I also like to listen and ask questions. [4]When I'm out at dinner with my dates, I make sure to ask them about their preferences, their interests, and their history. [5]Sometimes waiters don't refill our drinks frequently enough, but that's okay. [6]It's all

> **Paragraph Unity Tip**
>
> In this exercise and in your writing, it's a good idea to read a paragraph and see if you can summarize it in one sentence. If the paragraph had a headline, what would it be? In order to make sure the paragraph is unified around that idea, compare each of your sentences to your headline /summary sentence. Whatever doesn't relate should be moved or cut.

good. [7]If my dates don't ask about my interests, or if they don't listen when I'm speaking, I conclude that they are probably too self-absorbed or superficial for me. [8]Listening is very flattering, and it requires commitment, patience, and sympathy, which are qualities I admire greatly.

Paragraph 4:

[1]Filthy, foul-smelling vile work is what it is, but it sure does pay well. [2]Every day I wear work boots, jeans, protective gloves, a mask, and safety goggles so that the excrement doesn't make me ill or get on my skin. [3]Different people have different career interests. [4]Some of my friends work in offices. [5]I prefer to work outdoors. [6]Sometimes I have to walk in the muck, but usually my work is limited to dropping a vacuum hose in a cesspool, and letting the hose do the dirty work for me. [7]My friends laugh at me for having a career that is not glamorous and that affords almost no opportunities to meet attractive people, but at the end of the week I have the last laugh because I get paid twice as much as they do. [8]I spend a lot of my paycheck on payday, and most of that money goes to new video games and clothes.

Paragraph 5:

[1]Some people think that English is a Latin language, but it's really not. [2]While Latin did influence English, the most significant influence on the language was that of the lower west Germanic tribes that settled England. [3]Much of English vocabulary is Latin-based, but our vocabulary has more French than Latin according to many linguistic historians. [4]A lot of that vocabulary entered English in the latter parts of the medieval period when French was

very fashionable in England because, in part, English kings also ruled France. ⁵I love to read about the history of the language.

When to Create a New Paragraph

Exercise 3.6c
Creating Paragraphs

Directions: Read each passage and answer the questions.

> **New Paragraph Axioms**
>
> As a rule, create a new paragraph whenever you change **time**, **place**, or **topic**, and in dialogue, whenever you change **speaker**. For more on dialogue writing, see section 5.4.

Passage A:
How I Learned Where Paragraphs Begin and End

[1] There was I time when I didn't know when to end my paragraphs, so I just kept on writing and hoped nobody would notice. [2] Even though I knew that I was supposed to hit return and then tab in order to create a new paragraph, I didn't know when to do so. [3] Once in a while, when a paragraph was really long—like almost a page, I would create a new paragraph, but I didn't really feel sure about that method. [4] Eventually, I learned a few approaches that helped me with paragraphing. [5] First, it's important to read your paragraph and figure out what its main idea or topic is. [6] When you figure out the main idea, then you can tell if your paragraph should be reorganized into multiple paragraphs. [7] Since a paragraph is supposed to express only one main idea, create a new paragraph wherever the paragraph begins to discuss a different idea. [8] If you're writing about George Washington's military experiences and his political expertise in the same paragraph, you're

making a mistake. [9] A second instance in which you should create a new paragraph is when the paragraph shifts time or place. [10] If you're writing about breakfast and lunch in the same paragraph, for example, you might want to begin a new paragraph when you begin to discuss lunch, which is not only a separate topic, but also a distinct time. [11] One additional instance for creating new paragraphs pertains to dialogue writing. [12] Many writers don't know this, but whenever a new character speaks, create a new paragraph. [13] Now that I learned to read my paragraphs and ask whether I've changed topic, time or place, or if a new character is speaking, I feel more confident about where to begin and end a paragraph.

1. After which sentence should the writer begin a new paragraph?

   A. Sentence 2
   B. Sentence 5
   C. Sentence 8
   D. Sentence 9

2. The writer is considering dividing Passage A into two paragraphs and inserting a topic sentence at the beginning of the *second* paragraph. Which would most effectively serve as the topic sentence of that second paragraph?

   A. Writing paragraphs is very challenging.
   B. Composition theorists disagree about when to begin a new paragraph.
   C. Writing a good paragraph requires self-confidence.
   D. Although I used to be clueless about paragraphing, I now know a few techniques that really help me.

Passage B:
From Booker T. Washington's *Up from Slavery*

[1] In later years, I confess that I do not envy the white boy as I once did. [2] I have learned that success is to be measured not so much by the position that one has reached in life as by the obstacles which he has overcome while trying to succeed. [3] Looked at from this standpoint, I almost reached the conclusion that often the Negro boy's birth and connection with an unpopular race is an advantage, so far as real life is concerned. [4] With few exceptions, the Negro youth must work harder and must perform his tasks even better than a white youth in order to secure recognition. [5] But out of the hard and unusual struggle through which he is compelled to pass, he gets a strength, a confidence, that one misses whose pathway is comparatively smooth by reason of birth and race. [6] From any point of view, I had rather be what I am, a member of the Negro race, than be able to claim membership with the most favoured of any other race. [7] I have always been made sad when I have heard members of any race claiming rights or privileges, or certain badges of distinction, on the ground simply that they were members of this or that race, regardless of their own individual worth or attainments. [8] I have been made to feel sad for such persons because I am conscious of the fact that mere connection with what is known as a superior race will not permanently carry an individual forward unless he has individual worth, and mere connection with what is regarded as an inferior race will not finally hold an individual back if he possesses intrinsic, individual merit. [9] Every persecuted individual and race should get much consolation out of the great human law, which is universal

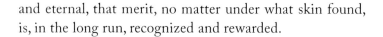

and eternal, that merit, no matter under what skin found, is, in the long run, recognized and rewarded.

1. After which sentence should the writer begin a new paragraph?

   A. Sentence 3
   B. Sentence 5
   C. Sentence 7
   D. Sentence 8

2. The writer is considering dividing Passage B into two paragraphs. Which would most effectively serve as the topic sentence of that second paragraph?

   A. Individual merit, not race, should be a person's primary source of pride.
   B. People who discuss race usually don't know what they're talking about.
   C. Race doesn't matter as long as a person is born healthy.
   D. Persecution is an important obstacle that enables people to reveal their individual merit.

Passage C:
From Aristotle's *Rhetoric*

[1] A speech has two parts. [2] You must state your case, and you must prove it. [3] You cannot either state your case and omit to prove it, or prove it without having first stated it. [4] Of these two parts the first part is called the Statement of the case, the second part the Argument. [5] These two parts are the essential features of a speech. [6] 'Refutation of the Opponent' is considered part of the

argument; so is 'Comparison' of the opponent's case with your own, for that process is a magnifying of your own case and therefore a part of the argument, since one who does this proves something. [7] The Introduction is the beginning of a speech, corresponding to the prologue in poetry and the prelude in music; they are all beginnings, paving the way, as it were, for what is to follow. [8] The musical prelude resembles the introduction to speeches of display; as musicians play first some brilliant passage they know well and then fit it on to the opening notes of the piece itself, the writer should proceed in the same way: he should begin with what best strikes his imagination, and then strike up his theme and lead into the Statement of the case. [9] And here in an Introduction, it is fitting for you to wander far from your subject rather than that there should be sameness in the entire speech.

1. After which sentence should the writer begin a new paragraph?

   A. Sentence 2 because here the paragraph changes subject
   B. Sentence 4 because here the paragraph changes time
   C. Sentence 6 because it just doesn't belong in the piece at all
   D. Sentence 7 because the paragraph shifts subjects from a discussion of speech parts in general to a more detailed discussion of one particular part of a speech.

2. The writer is considering dividing Passage C into two paragraphs. Which would most effectively serve as the topic sentence of that second paragraph?

A. Speeches need introductions.
B. An introduction serves rhetorical and stylistic purposes.
C. Introductions can be like music.
D. Introductions should wander from their subject.

Passage D:
From D. H. Lawrence's short story "The Horse Dealer's Daughter"

[1] He laid her down on the bank. [2] She was quite unconscious and running with water. [3] He made the water come from her mouth, and he worked to restore her. [4] He did not have to work very long before he could feel the breathing begin again in her; she was breathing naturally. [5] He worked a little longer. [6] He could feel her live beneath his hands; she was coming back. [7] He wiped her face, wrapped her in his overcoat, looked round into the dim, dark-grey world, then lifted her and staggered down the bank and across the fields. [8] It seemed an unthinkably long way, and his burden so heavy he felt he would never get to the house. [9] But at last he was in the stable-yard, and then in the house-yard. [10] He opened the door and went into the house. [11] In the kitchen he laid her down on the hearthrug, and called. [12] The house was empty. [13] But the fire was burning in the grate.

1. After which sentence should the writer begin a new paragraph?

   A. Sentence 3
   B. Sentence 4

C. Sentence 5
D. Sentence 9

2. In fiction writing, such as Passage D above, it's a good idea to begin a new paragraph...

A. When the setting changes (time or place)
B. When a new character speaks
C. When the topic changes
D. All of the above

23

TRANSITIONS

Transitions help readers to see relationships between ideas. Needed between sentences and paragraphs, transitions guide the reader from one point to the next. Transitions are two-faced, **looking backward** to an idea you just discussed, and **looking forward** to the next point you are about to make. They tell the reader what you discussed, and what you're about to discuss. Serving a **stylistic purpose**, transitions provide a smooth flow to writing. Performing a key **rhetorical function**, they emphasize key points and prepare readers for upcoming ideas. Transitions are very difficult to create since they require a writer to be in control of multiple parts of a composition, but for this very reason, transitions are very revealing about the quality of writing. An obvious sign of composition clarity, unity, and organization, a thoughtful transition shows readers and teachers how well you write, for in order to create an effective transition, writers must be able to describe what they just talked about and introduce what they are about to discuss all while clearly indicating the relationship between those two parts of the composition. It's not easy to make an effective transition, but when you do create a good one, the writing on both sides of the transition benefits.

The conventional way to create an effective transition between paragraphs is to use a transitional word/phrase + main idea of the previous paragraph/sentence + main idea of the current paragraph/sentence. In this way, if readers looked only at the transition, they should be able to deduce what you just talked about and what you're going to discuss.

Example: While Jones isn't the friendliest person, she is honest.

Note the three-part structure: **transitional word/phrase** (while, which signals a change is coming) **+ main idea of previous sentence/paragraph** (Jones unfriendly) **+ main idea of current paragraph** (Jones honest).

Broadly speaking, transitions function in three ways: (1) they show that you're <u>continuing or adding</u> to the direction of your sentence, (2) they show that you're <u>emphasizing</u> your ideas, or (3) they indicate that you're <u>changing</u> the direction of your ideas.

Common Transitions

Continue the direction	Emphasize	Change the direction
In addition	Indeed	Still
Moreover	In fact	Instead
Also	Certainly	Although
Furthermore		While
Therefore		However
Thus		Meanwhile
For example		In contrast
Consequently		Nevertheless
As a result		Usually
Similarly		Normally
Likewise		But
		Once
		Now

Transition Tips

1. Not every sentence or paragraph needs a transitional word/phrase. You can transition in other ways, especially by repeating ideas and finding words that resonate with the words/ideas in neighboring sentences and paragraphs.

2. Most writers place transitions in the first sentence of the next paragraph. Consider using transitions in the **last sentence** of a paragraph, which may very well create better flow.

3. Do NOT rely on bald transitional words/phrases to begin a new paragraph. Don't merely write *In addition*, *However*, etc; instead, use the transitional word/phrase + repetition of previous idea + introduction of new idea formula.

Look Back

See section 3.1 on Martin Luther King's "I Have a Dream" speech, which models alternate ways to transition.

Example: In addition to serving honorably as police commissioner, Teddy Roosevelt earned public respect for his work as governor. [Note how the transitional phrase (In addition) establishes a relationship between a previously discussed idea (honorable service as police service) and a new idea (earned respect as governor).

Exercise 3.7A Transitions between Sentences

Directions: Choose the word that creates the most effective transition within and between sentences.

1. In most cases, she does what she's asked. In this case, _____, she did not.

    A. therefore
    B. consequently
    C. similarly
    D. however

2. The scientist discovered that some of the experiments were flawed. _____, she believed that the experiments did have some value.

A. Nevertheless
B. Moreover
C. For example
D. In addition

3. He is a poor dribbler, erratic shooter, and soft defender. _____, he is the team's most skillful basketball player.

A. In fact
B. Instead
C. Still
D. Meanwhile

4. During the first four days, it rained while we vacationed in Florida. For the final three days, _____, it was hot and dry.

A. thus
B. in contrast
C. for example
D. consequently

5. The author makes a compelling case for the way to create jobs. She _____ demonstrates how to strengthen American foreign policy.

A. therefore
B. indeed
C. also
D. usually

6. There are several instances in which a writer should use a semicolon. _____, one could place a semicolon between two very closely related independent clauses.

A. For example
B. Likewise
C. Thus
D. Consequently

7. _____ I entered the classroom late, I asked the student next to me what I had missed.

A. After
B. Although
C. Meanwhile
D. Indeed

8. _____ it's perfectly acceptable to place transitions at the beginning of a paragraph, the end of a paragraph is also a suitable place for a transition.

A. Since
B. Moreover
C. Because
D. Although

9. When I was fourteen, I took a job at an ice cream shop to help my parents pay the bills. _____, I would help with the chores whenever I was asked.

A. Consequently
B. Moreover
C. Therefore
D. Moreover

10. _____ I finish my work on time. Today, I didn't.

A. Now
B. Usually

C. In fact

D. In contrast

Exercise 3.7b   Transitions between Paragraphs

Directions: Each of the questions contains the end of a paragraph and the beginning of the next paragraph. Choose the answer that most accurately evaluates the bolded transitions between paragraphs.

1.   The Superiority Theory of laughter is right in asserting that people laugh at others' misfortune. Some of us truly do enjoy it when we escape ridicule and when foolish people get what they deserve: humiliation that comes from derisive laughter. **Clearly we laugh out of a sense of superiority over those who are the target of humor, but that isn't the only reason we laugh: sometimes we laugh out of a sense of relief, as we often do when we are in tense situations**.

   The Relief Theory proposes that people laugh as a result of releasing excess nervous energy that accumulates during stressful moments.

   A. The bolded transitional sentence is effective because it highlights the current idea and introduces the new idea on the Relief Theory with words that resonate with each other.

   B. The bolded transitional sentence is ineffective because transitions should only be at the beginning of a paragraph, and this one is at the end of a paragraph.

2.   The "silent member" of the Continental Congress, Thomas Jefferson used his pen to advocate for individual liberty and against strong, centralized government. The Declaration of Independence, which he drafted when he was 33 years old, is, perhaps, his greatest written achievement.

In addition, Jefferson was a brilliant architect, who designed a masterful home atop Monticello and much of the University of Virginia, including the rotunda.

A. The transitional sentence is effective because of its reliance upon a useful transitional phrase that clearly establishes the relationship between the two paragraphs.

B. The transitional sentence is ineffective because it relies on a bald transition that does not clearly establish how the second paragraph relates to and builds upon the first.

3.   She didn't feel joy on her wedding day. Nothing registered in her heart when her first child was born. **She hadn't felt anything, in fact, since that autumn day when they consoled each other under a birch tree in the park.**

On a wooden bench beneath a canopy of ruddy birch leaves, he clasped her hands while a tear drop plodded down her face.

A. The transitional sentence is effective because much of its language resonates with and anticipates the language in the ensuing paragraph.

B. The transitional sentence is ineffective because it doesn't flow smoothly into the next paragraph.

4.   The American experiment in self-government nearly died in its cradle. Without ratification of the Constitution by nine of the original states, the United States may have died in its infancy. Convincing nine states to adopt the Constitution was not easy. **Ten months of written and oral debate between Federalists (supporters of the new Constitution) and Anti-Federalists (those opposed) seized the fledgling nation's attention, but no arguments were as eloquent or as persuasive as those that came to be known as *The Federalist Papers*.**

Written under the pseudonym Publius by Alexander Hamilton, John Jay, and James Madison, *The Federalist Papers* is considered the most accurate commentary on the intentions of the founders and among the most insightful documents about the debates between Federalists and Anti-Federalists.

A. The transitional sentence is ineffective because of its failure to employ a useful transitional word and failure to convey the relationship between the ideas in each paragraph.
B. The transitional sentence coherently links ideas between each paragraph through its use of repetitious language and logical flow of ideas.

5.   19th and early 20th-century doctors who sought to cure cancer often failed because of their misunderstanding of cancer's behavior and their inability to detect its movements. William Halsted's belief that surgery could cure breast cancer led him

and his disciples on a brutal quest to cut out as much of the chest and surrounding areas as possible in order to prevent the spread of cancer. His mastectomies were disfiguring and highly ineffective, for he did not understand that the cancer may have spread beyond the area he had removed long before his life-threatening surgeries.

Nevertheless, surgery wasn't as horrible as it had been, especially because of the use of anesthesia and insistence upon sterilizing tools and wounds.

A. The transitional sentence is ineffective because it does not relate at all to the ideas in the previous paragraph.

B. The transition effectively links the ideas between paragraphs by using words that reiterate the main idea of the previous paragraph and introduce the main idea of the current paragraph.

Part IV

CLARITY, COHESION, AND CREATIVITY IN TITLES, OPENINGS, AND CONCLUSIONS

Insightful Thesis Sentences, Effective Titles, Meaningful Openings, and Symmetrical Endings

Topics Covered in this Part

1. Composing effective titles
2. Techniques for writing a creative opening
3. How to produce a meaningful conclusion
4. Building effective thesis sentences

24

EFFECTIVE TITLES

Ideally, we wouldn't judge a book by its cover…but we do. If you've been persuaded by Malcolm Gladwell's *Blink*, you might agree that we do judge books by their covers—that split-second judgments based on seemingly fragmentary evidence can be as accurate as and more efficient than those decisions reached by careful deliberation.

And the fact is, **titles** are your first place to make an impression on the reader. If that reader is your teacher, you do not want the teacher to get the wrong split-second impression about a paper from a stale, thoughtless title. Instructors constantly evaluate your writing, trying to classify it according to various criteria. One of those areas that they examine is titles, which reveal whether the paper is **on task**, whether the composition promises to be **original**, and whether the writing is **cohesive.**

An effective title has the following qualities: (1) It **seizes the interest** of its audience and (2) It **previews the main idea** of the paper. Titles that effectively address only one of those aspects tend to be either absurd or flat, offering the reader a distorted view of the paper or diminishing the reader's eagerness to read on.

Make your titles count, make them more relevant by referring to them in the key places of the composition—especially in the beginning and end. Do this by choosing words and creating sentences that resonate with the words in your title. Note, for example, how Percy Shelley makes his title count in his poem "Ode to the West Wind." Throughout the poem, he incorporates many words that relate to the idea of "ode," which is a word that is rooted in the Greek word for song. Here are a few examples of words that resonate with the title's emphasis on song, with line numbers in parentheses: "clarion" (10), "hear" (14), "lyre" (57), "harmonies" (59), "incantation" (65), and in the line before the last line of the poem, "trumpet" (69).

An effective title makes a splash whose ripples are evident in every paragraph of the composition, flowing to the very end of the paper. The title resonates with the rest of the paper.

So when should you write a title? Believe it or not, a good title usually manifests late in the writing process. Why? Well if a title previews the main idea of a paper, how can you write a dazzling title before you've written the paper, or know what the main idea is? Consider writing the title near the middle or end of the writing process. However…and this is a big however…if you create a dazzling title early in the process, if you can use that creative title to organize and develop the paper.

AVOID THE FOLLOWING APPROACHES TO TITLES

1. No title. Yes, the number one error with titles is not to include a title. Take advantage of the opportunity titles provide for showing off your style and helping your reader to prepare for the main idea.
2. Do not write a title that poaches generalities from the assignment guidelines or the topic. Don't title your paper the same title as the text you're analyzing ("Hamlet" or "Of Mice and Men"). For example, if you're assigned a research paper on genetics, don't call your paper "Genetics" or "Research on Genetics." Don't write "Essay on _____" or "Story about _____."
3. In general, avoid titles that are vague or generalities—titles that anyone could have written and that do not specifically relate to your main idea. Do not title your paper, for example, "Different Views of Marriage," and don't title your paper "The Environment." These are very vague, unexciting, and provide very little insight about the paper topic.
4. Do not write a title that is a complete sentence.

EMBRACE THE FOLLOWING APPROACHES TO TITLES

1. Choose a title that resonates with a key word or phrase in the body of the paper. Make the title count by referring to it in the paper, especially at the beginning and end of the composition.
2. Consider using a **colon** in titles of essays, research papers, and response papers in order to be creative and

preview the main idea—that is, it's a good idea to refer to the text or topic of discussion in a subtitle after a colon. For example, "Nothing Is As It Seems: An Analysis of *Gulliver's Travels*."
3. When in doubt, choose a **specific** title rather than a general one.
4. Always try to create an interesting and relevant title.
5. Consider using a title that **puns**.

Exercise 4.1a Characteristics of Good Titles

<u>Directions:</u> Evaluate the titles in each cluster. Circle the letter that corresponds to the title that seems to be most effective. Be prepared to discuss why the titles you rejected aren't as effective as your final answer. Refer to the approaches above (Approaches to embrace and avoid in titles) in order to support your answers or why you eliminated a choice.

1. A student who wrote a narrative about an unpleasant family trip to Disney is considering the following titles. Which would be the most effective at previewing that main idea and seizing a reader's interest?

   A. My Family Trip to Disney
   B. Disney
   C. Captive in the Dungeons of Disney

2. A student who wrote an essay about people's inaccurate ideas about religion is considering the following titles. Which would be the most effective at previewing that main idea and seizing a reader's interest?

   A. Views of Religion

B. Chapter and Verse: Misconceptions about Religion

C. Religion

3. A student who wrote a research paper about ecological paradoxes is considering the following titles. Which would be the most effective at previewing that main idea and seizing a reader's interest?

A. The Naturalness of the Unnatural

B. Is Nature Good or Bad?

C. Nature Essay

4. A student who wrote a harsh review of the movie *Paranorman* is considering the following titles. Which would be the most effective at previewing that topic and seizing an audience's interest?

A. Critique of *Paranorman*

B. Paraboring

C. Die! Die! Die! A Movie for Idiots Only

5. A student who wrote a blog about fashion styles and the personalities of the celebrities wearing those fashions is considering the following titles. Which would be the most effective at previewing that topic and seizing a reader's interest?

A. My Thoughts about a Glamorous Night at the Oscars

B. Hollywood's Beautiful Celebration

C. Fashionably Churlish: Dress and Attitude at the Oscars

6. A student who wrote an essay about violence during the French Revolution is considering the following titles. Which would be the most effective at previewing that main idea and seizing a reader's interest?

   A. Robespierre and Despair: How a Righteous Revolution Turned Brutal
   B. Violence
   C. Essay on the French Revolution

7. A student who wrote a summary and response about racism in James Baldwin's short story "Going to Meet the Man" is considering the following titles. Which would be the most effective at previewing that topic and seizing a reader's interest?

   A. Response Paper on Baldwin
   B. Baldwin's Racist Story
   C. Going to Meet a Racist: Inherited Ideas about Racism in Baldwin's Short Story

8. A student who wrote a composition about her role within her family is considering the following titles. Which would be the most effective at previewing that topic and seizing a reader's interest?

   A. My Family
   B. My Place at the Table
   C. Love for Family

9. A student who wrote a reaction paper about magic in *Harry Potter and the Prisoner of Azkaban* is considering the following titles. Which would be the most effective

at previewing that main idea and seizing a reader's interest?

A. The Prison and Prism of Magic in *Harry Potter*
B. Magic
C. Reaction to Ideas about Magic in *Harry Potter*

10. A student who wrote an essay about media bias is considering the following titles. Which would be the most effective at previewing that main idea and seizing a reader's interest?

A. Bias in the Media
B. Lying Press
C. Mass Media's Mass Manipulation

25

MEANINGFUL OPENINGS

There is a tremendous burden on an opening to achieve two goals: seize the audience's *interest* and introduce the *main idea*. One additional but not as important objective is to *establish your credibility* on the subject you're discussing. Credibility (this writer has done her research, this writer knows facts associated with the topic, the writer has a command of the material, including knowledge of multiple opposing viewpoints, etc.) encourages readers to continue reading and to embrace your ideas.

Opening sentences, therefore, are exciting or controversial or unexpected or provocative, but they are always supposed to be insightful.

Emily Dickinson has a poem titled "Tell all the truth, but tell it slant." This is a useful way to think of openings. Get to the truth (main idea) indirectly, or diagonally. This indirect route to your main point affords you opportunities to seize the readers' interest and establish your credibility as readers advance through the opening paragraph.

There are many strategies for creating an effective opening, but in general, think about writing the beginning at some later point in the writing process. It's very difficult to produce an engaging opening that previews the main idea when you first start writing for the same reason it's difficult to create an effective title at the beginning of the writing process: very often, at the early stages of the writing process, you just don't know yet what your main point is.

Techniques to Embrace in Beginnings

1. Begin with a **list**. Packed with <u>energy and variety</u>, lists offer you a different way to open a paper. Lists work with many modes of composition, from creative writing to literary analysis and research papers. In creative writing, consider using the five senses in the lists. We tend to resort to the sense of sight. Try to make us hear, feel, taste, or smell as well. In essay and research writing, consider using lists of facts, historical moments or figures, and other information that establishes your knowledge of the subject and introduces main ideas.

Example of a list opening: I stuffed the backpack with my jock strap, stockings, cleats, jersey, and deodorant. I removed my cell phone, wallet, and keys from the small side pocket of the bag. On my way out of the locker room, I passed dozens of boys—some dressed, some getting dressed, some primping, some talking, some sitting quietly, and some, like me, headed toward the door. I smelled aerosol deodorant, cologne, toothpaste, urine, mildew, and must. My jeans scraped against the polished wooden benches and my backpack grazed the metal lockers as I squeezed past my teammates and pushed open the door.

2. Present and then refute an **opposing viewpoint**. Opening this way shows that you are fair (you consider other points of view), that you have a breadth of understanding of the subject (you know your ideas and the ideas of those who disagree with you), and that you are adroit with transitions since you must shift from one point to another in order to get from opposing view to your own viewpoint. This method also introduces conflict into the paper which contributes to the attention-grabbing potential of the writing. Finally, as John Stuart Mill points out in his book, *On Liberty*, there is probably no more important intellectual trait than the willingness to understand opposing viewpoints. When people and societies that are unwilling to seek out, and even embrace opposing viewpoints, there is no intellectual freedom for the writer, no equitable discussion of ideas for the reader, and there is no political freedom for the individual.

Example of an opposing viewpoint opening: He has been dismissed as an actor "playing president." He has been described as a "cowboy" with a reckless approach to foreign policy that nearly caused global nuclear war. His policies have been characterized as divisive, and he was even accused of ignoring the AIDS epidemic and turning a blind eye to the poor. Nevertheless, most objective surveys of presidents consistently rank Ronald Reagan in the top third of presidents because of his economic vision and foreign policy leadership.

CLARITY, COHESION, AND CREATIVITY

3. Use **negation**. Tell the reader what you're *not* going to talk about or what is *not* accurate about our understanding of your subject. Then segue to what you will discuss. Opening this way is unusual, so it appeals to readers' interest, and it allows you to frame your point through contrast.

Example of a negation opening: I don't like romantic walks at sunset or snuggling under the stars. I can't stomach public displays of affection or candle-light dinners. I don't want to hear how much I'm loved and I don't want to receive flowers or chocolates. But I do like to sit in front of the television on Sunday afternoons with my dog and a cold drink.

4. Provide an **anecdote**. Useful in a variety of genres, anecdotes grip us as little stories within our larger compositions. These little stories, at first, don't appear relevant, but as they unwind and approach the main idea, they reveal themselves to be gripping and relevant. Anecdotes are personal, so they help us to connect with readers and draw upon the universals we have in common. A good anecdote allows us to come at our main point indirectly, which generates suspense.

Example of an anecdote opening: After the divorce, my mother very capriciously decided when my father would be allowed in the house and when he wouldn't. With custody of us only on the weekends, but no visitation rights, my father would seize those rare Sunday night opportunities to tuck me in and tell me a story. Stories of adolescent dinosaurs that were separated from their parents or the magical bonds between a lonely young boy and a moth that lived in his closet are just two of the fictions my dad created to help me understand what he wanted for me: companionship and escape. What my father was trying to do with his stories is similar to what fairy tale critic Bruno Bettelheim prizes in the great fairy tales: their ability to serve as moral companions and escape mechanism for anxious children.

5. Discuss an **example, representative quote,** or **scene**. Choose a key scene or key line from the text you're analyzing and show how that line/scene epitomizes your point about the text you're analyzing. This technique shows that you can do a close textual reading and it establishes your command of the material.

Example of key quote/scene opening: Shelley's poem "Ode to the West Wind" plays with the ideas of the wind as both "Destroyer and Preserver." Shelley admires this paradoxical ability of the wind to destroy and preserve, and he wants us to submit willingly to our own figurative destruction so that we can preserve the better part of ourselves.

6. Choose an appropriate **part of speech** (verb if you want action, adverb/adjective if you want to describe, for example) or **narrative technique** (dialogue, flashback, etc.).

Techniques to Avoid in an Opening

A. Don't begin with a **definition**...unless you're going to refute or challenge the definition.

Readers don't need you to define what love is or to offer a definition of shyness. Stating the obvious will prevent an opening from grabbing our interest. If you feel the need to begin with a definition, do so if you're going to <u>disagree</u>, with or challenge that conventional definition.

Example of what *not* to do: Webster's Dictionary defines integrity as "firm adherence to a code." My grandpa was certainly a man of integrity.

B. Don't begin with a famous quote…unless you're going to do something meaningful or unexpected with the quote.

    Quotes aren't original, by definition, because you didn't create them. Quotes tend to be crutches for writers struggling to find an original opening. If you feel the need to begin with a quote, consider **disagreeing with the quote**.

Example of what *not* to do: Maya Angelou once said "Life loves the liver of it." I agree with her point and wish others would heed her good advice.

Better is to disagree with or challenge the quotation:
May Angelou once said "Life loves the liver of it." She may have been an insightful writer, but she's dead wrong in this case. How can you say life loves the liver of it when we live in a world in which so many children are abused and so many innocents are tortured?

C. Don't begin with a **generality**, especially one you're not qualified to make. **Avoid the obvious**.

"Often in life…" That phrase shouldn't begin a paper. There are those who believe that a paper should begin with the general and move to the specific. To the contrary! It's preferable to **begin with the specific** and get more specific. Even better is to begin with the specific and reason the general.

Example of what *not* to do: Often in life, we lose people whom we care about. I have lost a grandfather, two uncles, and a cousin. Losing people we care about hurts.

D. **Don't prematurely reveal the climax** in <u>creative writing</u>.

It's usually advisable to avoid revealing the significance and turning point of the story in your opening. Don't tell us that "This was going to be the worst day of my life," or "I had no idea my life was about to change forever," or "I will never forget the pain I felt on that day." This approach of giving away the ending and commenting on it is not effective.

Example of what *not* to do: It was a Friday morning when I decided to get my tattoo. I had saved the money, selected the image, and prepared my escape. This day was going to be the day that my life changed forever.

Other Suggestions:
When writing an essay that is based on a text (film, story, essay, book, etc.), you should, at some point in the introduction, identify the author(s) and title(s) of the text(s) you're analyzing.

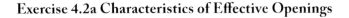
Exercise 4.2a Characteristics of Effective Openings

Directions: 1. Read each assignment. 2. Then evaluate the openings in each cluster: which is the better opening: A or B? 3. In the spaces below each cluster, (1) identify which techniques (technique to avoid or technique to embrace) each opening incorporates and (2) present your evaluation about which is the better opening: A or B? Refer to the techniques that commend your choice and discredit the other as "Techniques to Embrace" 1–6 and "Techniques to Avoid" A–D.

Assignment 1. You are the professor of an American literature course and you are preparing to return essays on Robert Frost's poem "Home Burial." You have the following two openings in front of you to use as model introductions. Which would you choose as the better model?

A. According to Helen Keller, "Death is no more than a passing from one room into another." Often in life, people die prematurely. When kids die, their parents are devastated. The death of a child is unnatural and rare. Nobody should have to deal with that kind of pain. In Robert Frost's poem "Home Burial," the husband and wife are deeply hurt by the unnatural pain of losing their child.

B. Sometimes I look out my window and stare at the empty swing in my backyard. I used to push my little brother on that same swing until very recently, when he passed away in a car accident. He was only four years old. Although I don't blame my mother, who was driving the car when he died, I can't help but be angry at her every time I look at that empty swing. Sometimes, when I hear the swing creaking in the wind, I get furious, holding her responsible and feeling like I could never forgive her. Robert Frost's poem "Home Burial" explores our need to blame someone when tragedy strikes, and Frost shows us how hard it is for people who love each other to forgive and recover when a loved one dies.

Assignment 2. You are the professor of a history class and you are preparing to return term papers on the Civil War. You have the following two openings in front of you to use as models introductions. Which would you choose as the better model introductory paragraph? Why? Be sure to discuss the weaknesses of the opening that you reject.

A. 1,100,000 casualties. 620,000 dead. 23,000 died in only two days at Shiloh. Why did so many sacrifice themselves to preserve the union? Why did so many give their lives to destroy it? In this paper, I will show how political rhetoric provides an answer to these questions, discussing how words, contrary to the sticks and stones aphorism, can indeed hurt individuals and a nation.

B. Someone once said that "War is hell." The Civil War was certainly a hellish war. Lots of people died. Americans killed Americans. We fought the war to make our country a better place, especially for slaves.

_____

_____

_____

_____

_____

Assignment 3. You are the professor of a composition class who is preparing to return papers. You have the following two openings in front of you to use as models. Which would you choose as the better model opening? Why? Be sure to discuss the weaknesses of the opening that you reject.

A. The day started out like any other day. The blue sky and bright sun promised that it would be a nice day, but as it turned out, this was going to be one of the worst days of my life. Terrible things happened that day. I'll never forget these things because they influenced the person who I am today. I learned a lot about myself from the pain I experienced. People can learn from pain.

B. My mother cracked the eggs and dropped them into the sizzling frying pan. I sat at the table, staring at the Knicks box score in the *Post*.

"Do you want any bacon?" she asked.

I looked up from the paper, told her "No thanks," and resumed reading. Someone rang the doorbell, which was unusual on a Friday at seven in the morning. I got up, walked toward the door, and looked through the peep hole. Two tall men wearing ski masks and gloves lurked on the other side of the door.

_____

_____

_____

_____

_____

Assignment 4. You are a professor in the Department of Communications preparing to return research papers. Which of the two openings below would you choose as the better model introductory paragraph? Why? Be sure to discuss the weaknesses of the opening that you reject.

A. People communicate for a variety of reasons. Some people communicate in order to learn information. Other people communicate in order to share what they know. What's most interesting about communication is the impact of the form of communication we use. My research shows that the form of communication affects the content of the message.

B. The average person spends more than an hour a day on the smart phone and almost twice that on the internet. Somehow, most of us have intuited something very subtle about the relationships between our mode of communication and the way our messages are received. When we talk on the phone, we can hear tone, but we can't see body language. And because speech is extemporaneous, we don't always have the time to formulate clearly-expressed ideas. When we communicate in writing, we can take all the time we need to find the right words, but writing is open to interpretation, and that ambiguity can create communication problems. What these examples illustrate is a truth about communication: the form of communication we use can affect the content of the messages we're trying to send.

26

SYMMETRICAL ENDINGS

The most neglected part of a composition, a **conclusion** is the forlorn step-child of the composition family. For some reasons, writers tend to neglect this important place, which serves crucial roles in a composition.

Conclusions offer writers one last opportunity to drive home their <u>main idea</u>. Conclusions also present writers with an opportunity to discuss the most meaningful and universal aspects of their writing—**why the ideas matter**. Conclusions should discuss the **broader significance** of the main idea of the paper. Go beyond mere reiteration of the main points and address the following questions: Why should the reader care about the points you're raising? So what? What would happen if your ideas weren't implemented? Why must the audience be aware of your main points? What feeling or impression do you want to leave the reader with: hope, despair, resolution, ambiguity, or some other feeling?

Beyond those rhetorical opportunities afforded by conclusions are the aesthetic aspects. Creating <u>symmetry</u> in compositions by bringing papers back to their beginnings, conclusions enhance the aesthetic value of your writing. The Harry Potter saga, for example, begins and ends with Voldemort trying to kill Harry. *Hamlet* begins and ends with a changing of the guard. *Finding Nemo's* opening and closing scenes take place in the anemone where Nemo and his father, Marlin, live. This symmetry can be created through contrast as well. Note, for example, how *Finding Nemo's* beginning and ending, although employing the same setting, reveal tremendous differences in Marlin's character, which has evolved from the overprotective father to the more encouraging and relaxed parent we see in the concluding anemone scene. So as you write, remember that conclusions look backward aesthetically, resonating with the beginning, and they look forward thematically, suggesting what the reader should feel and think about in the future.

Conclusions should achieve the following objectives:

1. They reiterate the **main idea**
2. They discuss the **broader significance** of the ideas
3. They **resonate with the opening** of the paper

What are some **approaches to use when composing an ending**?

1. **The Conventional Approach**
   Summarize your main points and discuss why they matter. Devote a considerable amount of time to discussing the broader significance of your ideas.

2. **Compare and Contrast**
   Consider revisiting your main points and their significance by comparing and contrasting them with other ideas.

3. **The Objection-Refutation Approach**
   This approach will allow you to speak to those who disagree with you and convince them that they should agree with you. Furthermore, by considering and refuting the opposing viewpoint, you can cleverly reiterate your main ideas, providing the conclusion with a certain degree of flair and intellectual honesty.

4. **Pose Questions**
   Try to pose a few questions that get at the heart of your composition. Don't ask yes/no questions; instead, pose higher-order questions that ask your reader to contemplate the significance of your ideas.

5. **Acknowledge limitations.**
   Conclusions don't have to be definitive. In fact, you'll have far more credibility with your reader if you acknowledge that you didn't research every aspect of the question, that you didn't read every relevant piece of scholarship, or that there are implications you haven't considered. What questions didn't you consider? Why? What impact might such gaps in learning have on your findings? Writing is not about finding *the* truth; it's about revealing *a* truth.

> **Art of the Conclusion**
>
> When writing an ending, always look back to the title and opening paragraph so that beginning and ending have symmetry. Try to connect the last paragraph to the first by letting the ending resonate with the language, ideas, settings, etc., of the opening.

Exercise 4.3a   Qualities of a Good Ending

<u>Directions:</u> Each cluster (A and B) is the ending of a composition. 1. Evaluate the endings. 2. Then circle the letter that corresponds to the more effective conclusion. 3. Be prepared to discuss which of the 5 approaches above are employed by the conclusions.

1. A.   Parents can be cruel, selfish, and worst of all, too often they can ignore their children. What we can we do to break this cycle of bad parenting? Why is it so important that we try?

1. B.   In conclusion, parents don't often treat their kids well. Parents are selfish, violent, and they don't pay enough attention to their children.

2. A.   Robert Moses was an arrogant man, but he accomplished so much during his lifetime. He built many roads, bridges, buildings and parks. Shea Stadium and Lincoln Center wouldn't have been built without him. Culture and entertainment are important for people, and we need roads and bridges to appreciate culture and to be entertained. Moses was truly a great man.

2. B.   Moses was arrogant and vain, and he clearly abused his power too often during his near half-century of influence. Nevertheless, or even because of these repugnant traits, he transformed New York's infrastructure and parks, building important bridges, such as the Verrazano, buildings, like Lincoln Center, and hundreds of parks and playgrounds. Should these

projects have been priorities? Did he use taxpayer funds to build what citizens needed or to erect an infrastructure that would glorify him? Regardless of the answers, these questions themselves reveal how divisive Moses was, and how divided scholars are about his legacy.

3. A. Overall, Sanders was a great coach whom I would love to have had. I'm sure that if he was my coach, no matter what the sport was, I would excel in it. He can turn anybody into a star athlete and push him on the right path to adulthood.

3. B. Sanders may have pushed his players too hard to achieve excellence. He probably yelled too much. Many players and parents complained that he was too intense for the high school level. While these criticisms might be justified, what's undeniable is that Coach Sanders showed his players how to live with intensity. That intensity, for Sanders, was crucial in ways that matter beyond the athletic field. Without intensity, there is no drive for academic success. Without intensity, there is no push for us to live with passion.

4. A. I've been arguing that we can improve composition instruction if we ask students to write more frequently and if we provide them with more timely feedback on their writing. One limitation of these suggestions is that they place a tremendous burden on all teachers, not just writing instructors, to do more work. In real life, there are very few people like Orwell's Boxer, who are willing to work harder than their colleagues for the same pay.

4. B. Reading writing, grading writing, and commenting on writing are time-consuming activities. So until we have a willingness on the part of our communities and learning institutions to invest more money into the teaching of writing or until we devise some other way of incentivizing those who devote the time and effort to grade writing, it's not likely that we will see better results. The amount of writing assigned probably won't increase, the amount of feedback will remain unfortunately constant, and quality of student writing will continue to lag.

27

INSIGHTFUL THESIS SENTENCES

Thesis Sentences

A thesis statement is a sentence that **expresses the main idea** of your paper. Think of it as a sentence that lays out what you want readers to learn by the time they finish reading the paper. You might also think of it as the answer to the question you posed when you began the writing process.

Thesis sentences usually do the following: (1) answer a question, (2) identify a problem, or (3) propose a solution to a problem or outline a course of action.

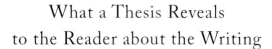

What a Thesis Reveals
to the Reader about the Writing

One of my former professors at the College of Charleston required students to write the following words on the front of papers: "The main point of this paper is that..."

What he was asking students to do was to read their papers so carefully, to become so familiar with their main ideas, that they could articulate their key points in one sentence. If a writer can't express the main point in one sentence, even if the composition is hundreds of pages long, then the writer doesn't know the idea well enough. And if the writer can't express the main idea in a sentence, then the reader certainly will be unlikely to comprehend the main idea. If you can't articulate the main point concisely, you don't have a command of the ideas, and your reader is less likely to understand your ideas.

Where do thesis statements go?

The conventional place for a thesis is at **end of the introductory paragraph**: let the thesis be the last sentence of the first paragraph. Master that strategy first.

Characteristics of effective thesis statements

Effective theses are insightful, debatable, and specific. After reading the thesis, the reader should learn something. Maybe it's about cause and effect, maybe it's about how something functions, maybe it's about the relationships between ideas, but either way, the thesis should be specific enough that a reader learns something after reading it.

If a thesis is too broad, for example, the reader will not learn and the writing will probably be vague.

Broad thesis: Playing sports has many benefits.

Better thesis: Sports improves physical health, builds social bonds, and fosters a sense of humility and discipline that are crucial for success.

Exercise 4.4a Effective Thesis Statements

Directions: Identify the most effective thesis statement in each question.

1A. George Washington was one of the greatest leaders in world history.
1B. George Washington's military experiences prepared him for the leadership demands of the presidency.
1C. Unlike most other presidents, George Washington was a general.

2A. Television has a variety of bad effects on viewers.
2B. Violence on television is ruining the soul of our country.
2C. Watching too much television can lead to obesity, mental health problems, and violent behavior.

3A. Children who don't receive enough attention from their parents are more likely to have low self-esteem, commit crimes, and become poor.

3B. Parents need to spend more time with their children.

3C. When parents neglect their children, the children suffer a variety of negative consequences.

4A. The main point of this paper is that Wordsworth's attitude toward the French Revolution changed from enthusiasm to disenchantment.

4B. Wordsworth's ideas about politics changed during his lifetime.

4C. William Wordsworth's views had many influences.

5A. Nineteenth-century American writers believed in freedom.

5B. In the early nineteenth century, American writers began to write about ideas that were universal.

5C. In the nineteenth century, American writers shifted from imitating European writers to creating a uniquely American type of writing.

6A. The Parthenon is an influential work of architecture.

6B. In order to understand the influence and functions of Classical architecture, one should study the Parthenon.

6C. The Parthenon architects were Ictinus and Callicrate, two of the more creative men in history.

7A. In 1609, Galileo observed moons orbiting Jupiter.

7B. Galileo's observation of moons orbiting Jupiter changed the world.

7C. Galileo's observation of moons orbiting Jupiter revolutionized our understanding of the solar system, religion, and our place in the universe.

8A. Charlemagne insisted that scribes copy and preserve the writings of Classical Rome.

8B. Charlemagne's insistence that scribes copy and preserve key writings of ancient Rome promoted developments in medieval literacy, architecture, and law.

8C. Charlemagne was an enlightened ruler even though he himself could not read or write.

9A. By applying Heisenberg's uncertainty principle and Bohr's ideas on the observer effect, I will demonstrate the inaccuracy and unreliability of eye witnesses.

9B. Heisenberg's uncertainty principle and Bohr's observer effect show us that there is a lot of unreliable information in the world.

9C. Heisenberg's uncertainty principle and Bohr's observer effect are important scientific principles.

10A. If we apply Joseph Campbell's ideas about the hero's journey to Orwell's novel *1984*, we can learn a lot about the main character, Winston.

10B. Joseph Campbell's theory about the hero's journey is applicable to so much literature.

10C. Campbell's theory suggests that because Winston does not complete the hero's journey, he should not be viewed as a hero, but as a failure.

Part V

TECHNICAL ASPECTS OF COMPOSITIONS

Topics Covered in This Part

1. Using quotes
2. Parenthetical citations
3. Formatting titles
4. Dialogue style and format

TECHNICAL ASPECTS OF COMPOSITIONS

Your parents, professors, bosses, and even you have particular ways that you prefer to have tasks completed. When you revise, make sure you conform to the technical demands of your writing assignment. Sometimes those demands come from instructors, sometimes they come from conventions and custom, and sometimes they come from the mysterious groups of people who determine how we must comply with those technical aspects. In most cases, especially in humanities classes, you'll be governed by the technical guidelines devised by a mysterious group known as the Modern Language Association, which is a club for scholars and teachers of English and foreign languages.

This section will address the following questions:

1. How and why should we quote for support?
2. Why do we need to parenthetically cite our sources and how do we do it?

3. What's the function of a works cited page?
4. How do I punctuate and effectively write dialogue?

28

SENTENCES THAT QUOTE EFFECTIVELY

Quotes allow you to show the reader **an example of the language that influenced your thinking**. They also serve to distinguish your words from the words of the sources you're quoting, which is the key for academic integrity. Quotes can be very persuasive and informative. When you quote for support, you're showing your readers language that you think is important and you're showing them why you think that language is important. The quotes are crucial for establishing that you read carefully and that you want your reader to know how the language you've quoted influenced your thinking.

Your professors and readers don't want to see too much quoting, however. If you quote excessively, or in the wrong manner, then you're asking your reader to do too much of the interpretive work. So quote only those relevant words that you can use to support the assertions you're trying to make. Consider the following when quoting:

1. Try to quote efficiently by **incorporating quotes into your sentences**.

Imagine that your literature professor asks a question on a homework or quiz about *The Odyssey* and requires a supporting quote. The professor asks the following: Why wasn't Poseidon at Olympus? <u>Your answer:</u> "He had gone to accept sacrifice of bull and rams, and there he sat and enjoyed pleasure of the feast" (Homer 3).

This method of quoting in big chunks, or creating an entire sentence out of a quote, is *not* helpful since the big chunks usually include irrelevant and distracting information. Your job is to eliminate unnecessary words—to be concise so that the reader understands. Your job is to translate the text for the reader. Don't make the reader translate for you.

Quote key words and **fuse them** with your words. A **better answer** to the question above on Poseidon: Poseidon was not at Olympus because he "had gone to accept a sacrifice" (Homer 3).

Note how this method combines quoted words with the writer's words while answering the question.

2. Don't quote **irrelevant parts** of the text.

Don't do this: Your professor asks a question on *The Odyssey*: Provide an example of a Homeric epithet. <u>Your answer:</u> One instance of a Homeric epithet in *The Odyssey* is when Homer says "Bright-eyed Athene answered him: 'Father of ours, Son of Cronos, King of Kings, if it is now the pleasure of the blessed gods that the wise Odysseus shall return to Ithaca, let us send our Messenger, Hermes" (Homer 5).

This response, of an entire sentence of quote, includes irrelevant information that might confuse the reader, so quote the relevant parts only to produce a better answer: One instance of a Homeric epithet is in *The Odyssey* when Homer describes Athene as "Bright-eyed Athene" (Homer 5).

Note how this method of quoting little bits of key words and integrating those little bits into your sentence allows you to clearly and concisely present your ideas and how the reading influenced your thinking. The reader doesn't have to interpret too much of the quoted text. You've contextualized the quote for the reader and eliminated extraneous words from the quotes, which prevents confusion.

Exercise 5.1a   Using Supporting Quotes

Directions: Each question provides a context that includes a course you're taking, a reading and writing assignment, and an excerpt from the assigned reading. Answer the question by quoting from the relevant parts of the assigned reading and by using the methods discussed at the beginning of this chapter.

1. On a quiz, your Freshman Seminar professor asks you to answer the following question on Dave Ellis' *Becoming A Master Student.*

Question: What are the three parts of the note-taking process? Quote from the reading for support.

This is the relevant quote from the reading that you want to use to support your response to the question: "Effective note taking consists of three parts: observing, recording, and reviewing. First, you observe an event—a statement by an instructor, a lab experiment, a slide show of an artist's works, or a chapter of required reading. Then you record your observations of that event; that is, you take notes. Finally, you review what you have recorded" (Ellis 149).

In the space below, incorporate and cite quotes to answer the question:

_____

_____

_____

_____

_____

_____

2. For homework, your history professor has asked you to answer the following question on Joseph Ellis' book *His Excellency, George Washington.*

Question: What was Washington's most important job? Quote from the reading for support.

This is the relevant quote from the reading that you want to use to support your response to the question: "Washington's highest duty was not to answer his critics or satisfy his sense of personal honor, but rather to win the war" (Ellis 108).

In the space below, incorporate and cite quotes to answer the question:

_____

_____

_____

_____

_____

_____

3. Your Sociology professor has asked you to address the following prompt on Barry Sanders' book *Laughter as Subversive History.*

Prompt: Identify a role of the jester, or joke maker. Quote from the reading for support.

This is the relevant quote from the reading that you want to use to support your response to the question: "The jester can retaliate as effectively as a flamethrower, not just by venting his anger, but by carefully aiming it, perhaps at the most vulnerable, or the most handy target, namely the person who has stumbled, or worse yet, the one who stands precariously off balance. The jester attempts to educate and purify with his fiery tongue. He does not set out simply to punish. And so the jester becomes a force to be reckoned with—a teacher and a judge" (Sanders 78).

In the space below, incorporate and cite quotes to answer the question:

_____

_____

_____

_____

_____

_____

4. Your English professor has asked you to answer the following question on D.H. Lawrence's short story, "The Rocking Horse Winner."

Question: How does the mother feel about her children? Quote from the reading for support.

This is the relevant quote from the reading that you want to use to support your response to the question: "She married for love, and the love turned to dust. She had bonny children, yet she felt they had been thrust upon her, and she could not love them. They looked at her coldly, as if they were finding fault with her. And hurriedly she felt she must cover up some fault in herself. Yet what it was that she must cover up she never knew. Nevertheless, when her children were present, she always felt the centre of her heart go hard. This troubled her, and in her manner she was all the more gentle and anxious for her children, as if she loved them very much. Only she herself knew that at the centre of her heart was a hard little place that could not feel love, no, not for anybody" (Lawrence 1).

In the space below, incorporate and cite quotes to answer the question:

_____

_____

_____

_____

_____

_____

29

USING PARENTHETICAL CITATIONS

When you do research or quote text, it's important for you to cite the source of your quotes and research. There are a variety of ways to cite quotes, but this chapter will focus on the method recommend by the Modern Language Association (MLA). **Parenthetical citations** provide you with a non-distracting way to help readers distinguish between your ideas and others' ideas. Rather than ask that you provide an entire bibliographic entry every time you quote or paraphrase the ideas of others, parenthetical citations ask for a minimal of information to be cited. Quotes distinguish your words and ideas from someone else's; citations identify, briefly, the source of others' words and ideas.

Here's an **example** of a sentence with an entire bibliographic entry in the parentheses:

> The King of Brobdingnag believes that Europeans are the "most pernicious race of little odious vermin"

ever to appear on earth (Swift, Jonathan. *Gulliver's Travels*. London: Penguin, 2003).

Here's an **example** of a sentence with the basic MLA information:

The King of Brobdingnag believes that Europeans are the "most pernicious race of little odious vermin" ever to appear on earth (Swift 123).

Notice how the latter example does not present as much distracting information as the first. It provides author's last name and page number, acting as a minimally intrusive invitation to the reader to visit the works cited page if the reader wants to learn more about the source that the writer is referring to.

What to Include in Parentheses

1. If you are **citing prose** (novel, essay, short story, newspaper, journal, etc.), provide the author's last name and the page numbers(s) on which the quotes appear.

   Example: (Cervantes 24).

2. If you are **citing poetry**, provide the poet's last name and the line number of the quote.

   Example: (Wordsworth 24).

Content of parentheses

1. Note how the period goes **after** the citation.

2. Note what's **not** in the parentheses: no pg; no#; no comma.

3. If you are citing a work with **multiple authors** but

fewer than three, include the names of all authors and the page number of quote. If there are more than three authors, include the author whose name appears first alphabetically, the phrase et al., and page number).

> **Example:** multiple authors, but fewer than three: (Aldo, Betamin, Carr 24).
> **Example:** more than three authors:
> (Anderson et al. 8).

4. When citing a website, provide the author and page number of the website. If no author is provided, include only the main part of the URL (cnn.com) as opposed to the complete URL (http://www.cnn.com). Consult with your professor since website citations change frequently and different professors have different rules about citing.

5. When citing the **Bible**, indicate the Book, chapter, a colon, and then the verse.

> **Example:** (Genesis 4:3).

6. When citing **Shakespeare's plays**, or other poetic plays, cite in the form of Act.scene.line#.

> **Example:** (Shakespeare V.ii.78–80).

*If a quote covers two or more pages of prose, or if a quote covers multiple lines of a poem, use the following technique.

> **Example prose:** (Dreiser 84–85).
> **Example poetry:** (Whitman 74–80).

*If you identify the author(s) in the sentence, you do *not* need to include their names in the parenthetical citations.

> **Example:** In his essay, Bevington discusses the historical context of Shakespeare's life and plays by noting that his activities from 1585–1592 are "wholly unknown" (7).

Exercise 5.2a   Using Parenthetical Citations

Directions: Indicate whether the citations are correct or incorrect. Then correct the citations if they require edits.

1. A student cited a quote from line twenty four of John Keats' poem "When I Have Fears That I May Cease To Be" in the following way: (Keats 24).

2. A student cited a quote from line twenty of William Butler Yeats' poem "The Stolen Child" in the following way: (William Butler Yeats line 20).

3. A student cited a quote from page seven of an article by Bill Jones titled "New Concerns About Links Between Bad Grammar and Bad Breath." The article appeared in *The New England Journal of* Medicine and the student cited the quote in the following way: [Jones pg 7]

4. A student cited a quote from pages eleven and twelve of Henry James' short story "The Pupil" in the following way: (Henry James, "The Pupil" pages 11-12).

5. A student cited a quote from page seventy-four of a textbook with two authors, Silverstein and Bowers, in the following way: (Silverstein et al. 74).

6. A student cited a quote from a website with an unknown author in the following way: (http://www.rdk.jones.van.com).

7. A student introduced a quote from the Biblical book of Leviticus in the following way: (Leviticus chapter 9 verse 2).

8. A student included a quote from page five of an article in *The Journal of Wretched Prose.* The article has four authors: Lahiri, Frey, Gallagher, and Jones. This is how the student cited the quote: (Frey, Gallagher, Jones, and Lahiri 5).

9. A student included a quote from Act Two, scene four, lines 126-131 of Shakespeare's *Measure for Measure.* The quote is on page 421 and the writer presented the citation in the following way: (Shakespeare 421).

10. A student quoted from page three of D. H. Lawrence's short story, "The Horse-Dealer's Daughter" and cited the quote in the following way: (Lawrence 3).

30

FORMATTING TITLES

In order to help your reader, you must present titles you refer to by using either quotation marks or italics. In general, titles of works that originally appear within larger works go inside quotes and the larger work is italicized. For example, an article in *The New York Times* would appear in quotes, but *The New York Times*, the larger work, is italicized. Learn when each is needed by reviewing the following lists:

Italicize the following titles:

- Books, such as *A Brief History of Time*
- Novels, such as *Great Expectations*
- Plays, such as *Hamlet*
- Long poems, such as *The Odyssey*
- Newspapers, such as *The New York Post*
- Speeches, such as *The Gettysburg Address*
- Magazines and journals, such as *Sports Illustrated*
- Album/CD titles, such as *Abbey Road*
- Television series, such as *The Big Bang Theory*

Put <u>quotes</u> around the following:

- Short stories, such as "The Birthmark"
- Essays, such as "The Lost Art of Argument"
- Newspaper articles, such as "Men Walk on Moon"
- Journal/magazine articles, such as "To Cheat or Not to Cheat"
- Song titles, such as "Here Comes the Sun"
- Television episodes, such as "Homer the Moe"

*Bear in mind that these rules apply to MLA style and not other styles such as APA. For example, using APA style, one would use quotes, not italics, around book titles.

Exercise 5.3A Title Format

<u>Directions:</u> Decide whether the title should be italicized or surrounded by quotes. Write *italicized* or *quotes* on the line near the title.

1. The Joshua Tree, a CD by the band U2.

   _____

2. Man Jumps into River to Save Drowning Boy, an article in a newspaper. _____

3. Cosmos, a book about the universe by Carl Sagan.

   _____

4. The Wreck of the Edmund Fitzgerald, a song by Gordon Lightfoot. _____

5. Long Day's Journey Into Night, a play by Eugene O'Neill.
   _____

6. The Wall Street Journal, a newspaper.
   _____

7. How Children Acquire Language, a chapter from a journal. _____

8. Dexter, a television series. _____

9. I Have a Dream, a speech by Martin Luther King.
   _____

10. The Great SAT Swindle, a novel by Mike Hartnett.
    _____

31

HOW TO WRITE DIALOGUE

Dialogue introduces diversity of narration into a composition. It tends to be more concise than narration, affording the writer a different approach to generating insights about the speaker and auditor of the dialogue. There are a few technical requirements for writing dialogue.

Rules for Punctuating Dialogue

1. Distinguish among <u>dialogue</u> (words spoken aloud to others), <u>inner monologue</u> (thoughts/words not spoken), and <u>indirect dialogue</u> (reports of what others say).

   A. Use <u>quotes</u> around dialogue.

   > **Example:** "I don't think I can hold it any longer, Mom. Please stop at the next rest area or my kidneys will burst."

   > Clearly, these words are spoken by one character to another, so the spoken words belong in quotes.

B. Place <u>thoughts that aren't spoken</u>—or words spoken only to one's self—in *italics*.

Example: *I don't think I can hold it any longer. That rest area had better be close.*

By italicizing these words, the writer is indicating that she thought the words, but did *not* speak them aloud.

C. Do <u>not</u> use quotes around indirect dialogue.

Example: He told me that he likes you.

2. <u>Capitalize</u> the first letter of dialogue, treating it as you would the beginning of a sentence.

Example:
"Where is the bathroom?" he asked.
He asked, "Where is the bathroom?"

3. <u>Dialogue interruptions</u> are *not* followed by capitals and usually are divided by dashes. Spoken words go inside the quotes, but the description of them, (action, or thoughts) is set off by dashes.

Example: "When will you learn"—he said as he stabbed his finger at the boy—"to be grateful for the things you have?"

4. Use <u>commas</u> between dialogue and tags (words that identify the speaker or the descriptions of the dialogue). But see rule 5 below for contradictory information, because sometimes other punctuation intervenes between dialogue and tags.

   Example: "You'd better not forget to wash your hands," she ordered.
   He moaned, "Please bring me some toilet paper."

5. Commas, question marks, and exclamation points go <u>inside quotes</u>. Periods go inside quotes when the dialogue ends the sentence.

   Example: "Hurry!" he begged, hoping she would exceed the speed limit.
   "Do you really have to go that bad?" she asked skeptically.

6. Quotes within dialogue need a single apostrophe to distinguish between what characters say and others' words.

   Example: "My mother always says 'Go before you go' to remind me to use the bathroom before I travel anywhere."

7. Any time a <u>speaker changes</u>, create a <u>new paragraph</u>.

   Example: At that time, Rick thought of a humorous anecdote. "My father-in-law has a funny way of describing cheap, ineffective toilet paper. Whenever I think about it, I crack up."

"What does he say? Tell me."

Laughing as he recalled the description, Rick said, "He calls that type of toilet paper 'Charles Bronson' because it's as tough as nails and doesn't take sh— from anyone."

Note how the new paragraphs are indented to indicate shifts in speakers.

Thoughts on Dialogue Style

1. Use effective words in **tag lines**. Don't rely on "said" if the character is yelling. Adjectives and adverbs are key, so **be precise**.

2. Use adjectives and adverbs effectively when writing tags, but try to let the dialogue speak for itself. If written well, the tone of the dialogue will be obvious to the reader, and tag lines, therefore, can be unnecessary or awkward.

3. It's not necessary to identify the speaker in every instance and tag. Let the reader glean speakers from context. Sometimes, intentionally withholding the identity of the speaker can create a healthy ambiguity. A tag line is not necessary every time a character speaks.

"Get over here."

"But I don't want to."

"Get over here now," his mother repeated.

"Fine"—he huffed—"but I don't understand why you always single me out."

Exercise 5.4a   Dialogue Writing

<u>Directions:</u> Identify the sentence that correctly punctuates and describes the dialogue.

1.   He asked her why she was so distant.

    A. "He asked her why she was so distant."
    B. *He asked her why she was so distant.*
    C. 'He asked her why she was so distant.'
    D. No change

2.   "Look out"! he said.

    A. "Look out!" he said to himself from across the room.
    B. "Look out!" he shouted from across the room.
    C. He said, "look out!"
    D. No change

3.   "Stop staring at me." "I'm not staring at you, you egotistical jerk," he protested indignantly. "Yes you are."

    A. "Stop staring at me."
       "I'm not staring at you, you egotistical jerk he protested indignantly."
       "Yes you are."
    B. *"Stop staring at me." "I'm not staring at you, you egotistical jerk," he protested indignantly. "Yes you are."*
    C. "Stop staring at me."
       "I'm not staring at you, you egotistical jerk," he protested indignantly.
       "Yes you are."
    D. No change

4. "I wonder why you get so angry anytime I ask you about your mother" The psychiatrist mused?

   A. "I wonder why you get so angry anytime I ask you about your mother"? The psychiatrist mused.
   B. "Why do you get so angry when I ask you about your mother?" the psychiatrist mused.
   C. "Why do you get so angry when I ask you about your mother"? the psychiatrist asked.
   D. No change

5. The detective looked at the photos. A series of questions formed in his mind. "Why does the body lack bruises? Why did she let the killer in the house?"

   A. The detective looked at the photos. Two questions nagged him, and he couldn't help but think about them. "*Why does the body lack bruises? Why did she let the killer in the house?*"
   B. The detective looked at the photos. Two questions nagged him, and he couldn't help but think about them. *Why does the body lack bruises? Why did she let the killer in the house?*
   C. The detective looked at the photos. Two questions nagged him, and he couldn't help but think about them. "Why does the body lack bruises"? "Why did she let the killer in the house"? he thought to himself?
   D. No change

6. [1] "Will this be the last time we see each other?" [2] "Let's not talk about it," he responded coolly. [3] "But I must know. If it is our last night, then everything is

different," she insisted. [4] "What difference does it make? Let's just let loose and forget about everything."

A. Create separate paragraphs for sentences 2, 3, and 4 because the dialogue speakers change at each of those locations.
B. Create a separate paragraph for sentence 2 only.
C. Create a separate paragraph for sentences 2 and 4 only
D. No change

7. "You should shut your mouth," the big man said.

A. Change "said" to "growled" because "growled" is a more revealing tag.
B. Change "big" to "old" because old people are usually angry about something.
C. Change "said" to "requested" because "requested" is a more sophisticated word that has associations of politeness that work well with this dialogue.
D. No change

8. "My professor always says, "Save your work often."

A. "My professor always says, 'Save your work often.'
B. "My professor always says, 'Save your work often.'"
C. "My professor always says, *Save your work often.*
D. No change

9. He looked her in the eyes. She searched his face for a clue, for a sign of hope that he would finally pop the question. His lips moved. He spoke. "Pass the ketchup, darling."

A. He looked her in the eyes. She searched his face for a clue, for a sign of hope that he would finally pop the question. His lips moved and he said, "pass the ketchup, darling."

B. He looked her in the eyes. She searched his face for a clue, for a sign of hope that he would finally pop the question. His lips moved. He spoke. Pass the ketchup, darling.

C. He looked her in the eyes. She searched his face for a clue, for a sign of hope that he would finally pop the question. His lips moved. He spoke, "*Pass the ketchup, darling.*"

D. No change

10. "Pick up your clothes. Put the Wii away and leave the remotes on the charger. Then brush your teeth. She is in one of those moods, he thought.

A. "Pick up your clothes. Put the Wii away and leave the remotes on the charger. Then brush your teeth." *She is in one of those moods*, he thought.

B. "Pick up your clothes. Put the Wii away and leave the remotes on the charger. Then brush your teeth." "She is in one of those moods," he thought.

C. Pick up your clothes. Put the Wii away and leave the remotes on the charger. Then brush your teeth. "She is in one of those moods," he thought.

D. No change

ANSWER KEY

Exercise 1.1a: Identifying Verbs
1. A
2. golden (adjective), car (noun), bold (adjective), filthy (adjective)
3. A
4. normally (adverb), yesterday (adverb), ferocious (adjective), old (adjective), orange (adjective)
5. B
6. under, near, by, with, for, and to (prepositions); women (noun)
7. A
8. slowly, carefully, defiantly, and definitely (adverbs)
9. Answers vary. Consider the following: draft, scrawl, pen
10. Answer vary. Consider the following: say, yammer, narrate

Exercise 1.1b: Subjects and Verbs in Context

1. C
2. C
3. B

4. A
5. B
6. C
7. C
8. A
9. B
10. C

Exercise 1.1c: More Subjects and Verbs

1. Verb: drove; Subject: I
2. Verb: is; Subject: She
3. Verbs: studies, is; Subjects: Spencer (subj. of *studies*), he (subj. of *is*)
4. Verb: causes; Subject: Arguing
5. Verbs: chugged, belched, angered; Subjects: I (subj. of *chugged* and *belched*), belched (subj. of *angered*)
6. Verbs: laughed, cried, screamed, heard; Subject: She
7. Verbs: knew, was: Subjects: I (subj. of *knew*), professor (subj. of *was*)
8. Verbs: smells, percolating: Subject: Nothing
9. Verb: is; Subject: softshell turtle
10. Verbs: was, watching, tearing, cursing; Subject: Sancho

Exercise 1.2a: Identifying Prepositions

1. B
2. toss (verb), slowly (adverb), uncle (noun)
3. A
4. press (noun or verb), solemn (adjective), potato (noun), door (noun), like (adjective, verb, or noun, depending on context)
5. Answers vary

6. No
7. Preposition and Object
8. Noun or a pronoun
9. a. snow b. soaring high c. drove d. played
10. Answers vary

Exercise 1.2b: Distinguishing Prepositional Phrases, Subjects, and Verbs

1. **PP:** of the proceeds; for food and clothing
   V: will be allocated
   S: portion
2. **PP:** On Saturday; to the mall; with Rick and John; for the concert
   V: am going; to buy
   S: I
3. **PP:** on the lampshade; by a cigarette; in the ashtray
   V: were produced; left
   S: stains (subj. of *were produced*); you (subj. of *left*)
4. **PP:** of the cradle; from your sad memories
   V: sing
   S: I
5. **PP:** in the kitchen; on the counter; near the microwave; alongside the cookie jar
   V: will find
   S: you
6. **PP:** in the summer
   V: like; drink; eat
   S: I
7. **PP:** along with two; of his annoying friends; with me; to the mall; on Friday
   V: went; to buy
   S: brother

8. **PP:** Across the street; from my house
   V: lives
   S: Boo Radley
9. **PP:** upon the brimming water; among the stones
   V: are
   S: nine and fifty swans
10. **PP:** into the wrong vein; from my arm; beneath my skin
    V: stuck, flowed, jabbed
    S: nurse (subj. of *stuck*); blood (subj. of *flowed*); she (subj. of *jabbed*)

Exercise 1.2c:
Identifying Subjects, Verbs, and Prepositions

1. A
2. A
3. A
4. A
5. B
6. B
7. A
8. B
9. A
10. B

Exercise
1.3a: Identifying Nouns

1. B
2. decide (verb), with (preposition), admit (verb), cloudy (adjective)

3. B
4. was (verb), examine (verb), near (preposition), from (preposition), injure (verb)
5. Answers may vary. Consider the following: research, registrar, tuition, dormitory

1.3b: Classifying Nouns

1. Verbal
2. Concrete
3. Proper
4. Abstract
5. Concrete
6. Concrete
7. Verbal
8. Proper
9. Abstract
10. Abstract

1.3c: Identifying Nouns in Context

1. Rivera, game, Yankees
2. milk
3. clouds, skies
4. roof, man
5. children, presents, Santa
6. frogs, toads, amphibians
7. Sunglasses, rays
8. Ice cream, cookies, cake, pudding
9. man
10. Gulliver, fire

* A and B: Answers vary

1.4a: Identifying Pronouns

1. A
2. with (preposition), under (preposition), for (preposition), from (preposition), belch (verb)
3. A
4. A
5. B

Exercise 1.4b: Pronouns and Their Antecedents

1. mother
2. dad
3. dish
4. Mike
5. sun
6. decisions
7. I
8. wall
9. He
10. the six hundred

Exercise 1.5a: Identifying Adjectives and Adverbs

1. B
2. patiently (adverb), hamburger (noun), under (preposition), carefully (adverb), throw (verb)
3. B
4. eager (adjective), perception (noun), soup (noun), shrewd (adjective), ugly (adjective)

5. A and B: Answers may vary

Exercise 1.5b: Adjectives and Adverbs in Context

1. T
2. T
3. A
4. B
5. B
6. A
7. A
8. B
9. A
10. B

Exercise 1.5c: More Adjectives and Adverbs

1. Adv: arrogantly
    Adj: vengeful
2. Adj: unrelenting
3. Adj: Faithful
4. Adv: jealously
5. Adv: Eventually, courageously
    Adj: resourceful
6. A. Adjective
    B. Claudius
7. A. Adverbs
    B. occasionally modifies contemplates; persistently
    modifies taunts
8. A. Adjective
    B. Hamlet
9. A. Adverb
    B. stabs

10. A. Adjective
    B. Claudius

* Answers may vary

Exercise 1.6a: Identifying Dependent and Independent Clauses

1. IND
2. D
3. IND
4. IND
5. D
6. D=underlined
7. IND=underlined
8. D=underlined
9. D=underlined
10. IND=underlined

*Answers may vary

Exercise 1.7a: Conjunctions

1. C
2. C
3. B
4. C
5. C
6. A
7. B
8. A
9. C
10. B

Exercise 2.1a: Identifying Run-Ons

1. A
2. B
3. A
4. B
5. B

Exercise 2.1b: Identifying Comma Splices

1. A
2. B
3. A
4. B
5. A

Exercise 2.1c: Identifying Fragments

1. A
2. A
3. A
4. B
5. A

Exercise 2.1d:
Correcting Splices, Run-ons, and Fragments

1. He is nice; she is not.
2. My brother always calls me on my birthday, but I sometimes forget to call him.
3. Beneath the table you'll find a pair of scissors. Be careful because they are sharp.

4. Texting while someone is trying to speak to you is rude. I hope you never do that again.
5. Mississippi Map turtles are native to the south, but they have been found as far north as Ohio.
6. Laurie never says hello to me when she's with the popular kids, which annoys me.
7. Answers vary: Pursuing my dreams with all my heart and soul will bring me success.
8. Rico loves to dance and chat with the ladies.
9. I probably won't come over tonight to watch the game, especially if you don't provide pizza and soda.
10. The number that you dialed is incorrect, so please check the number and dial again.

Exercise 2.1e:
Splices, Run-ons, and Fragments in Context

1. A
2. B
3. B
4. B
5. B

6. C
7. C
8. A
9. B
10. B

Exercise 2.2a: Subject-Verb Agreement

1. enjoys
2. is
3. thanks
4. argue
5. were
6. has
7. is

8. feel
9. are, distinguish
10. make

Exercise 2.2b:
Agreement Errors with Prepositional Phrases

1. draw; PP=on my car
2. is; PP=of homes
3. have; PP=about George Washington
4. has; PP=of the production, consumption, and transfer; 2nd PP=of wealth
5. was; PP=of weapons
6. is; PP=of birds and butterflies
7. has; PP=with scales
8. opens; PP=of keys
9. leads; PP=of many ships
10. deserves; PP=along with the owners

Exercise 2.3a: Tense Formation

1. drive
2. makes
3. planted
4. defeated
5. will steal
6. will copy
7. have worked
8. has been
9. had been
10. had earned
11. will have died
12. will have ended

Exercise 2.3b: Tense Identification

1. future perfect
2. present perfect
3. present perfect
4. future
5. past
6. present perfect
7. present
8. future perfect
9. past perfect
10. future
11. present
12. future
13. past perfect
14. future perfect

Exercise 2.3c: Tense Shifts and Errors

1. B
2. C
3. C
4. B
5. A
6. A
7. C
8. A
9. A
10. A

Exercise 2.4a: Pronoun Agreement

1. Ant=person; incorrect
2. Ant=group; correct or incorrect: do you want to treat the group as singular (one group) or refer to the group as many individuals (plural)?
3. Ant=coach; incorrect
4. Ant=Everyone; incorrect
5. Ant=person; correct, but try not to use gender specific pronouns in such cases. Make the antecedent (person) plural (people) and change the pronoun to they.
6. Ant=dog and cat; incorrect
7. Ant=representative; incorrect
8. Ant=person; incorrect
9. Ant=conference; incorrect
10. Ant=Wal-Mart; incorrect

*Answers vary on Question A

Exercise 2.4b: Pronoun Case

1. A
2. A
3. B
4. A
5. B
6. C
7. B
8. A
9. A
10. C

Exercise 2.4c: Pronoun Reference Errors

1. he
2. she
3. This
4. They
5. It
6. this
7. That
8. they
9. those
10. them

*Answers vary on Question A

Exercise 2.4d: Pronoun Shifts

1. C
2. A
3. D
4. A
5. C
6. A
7. D
8. D
9. C
10. D

*Answers vary on Question A.

Exercise 2.5a: Parallel Structure

1. B
2. A
3. A
4. C
5. A
6. A
7. B
8. A
9. C
10. A

*Answers vary in questions A-C.

Exercise 2.6a: Modifier Errors

1. B
2. A
3. C
4. A
5. B
6. A
7. C
8. B
9. A
10. B

Exercise 2.6b: More Modifier Errors

1. Protected by thick skins and sharp reflexes, the Mongoose has unique characteristics that enable it to kill the cobra.
2. Like most people, horses desire companionship.
3. Because their shells are hinged, box turtles can completely enclose themselves.
4. Camouflaging their skin, remaining still, and sacrificing their tails are just a few abilities that lizards have evolved in order to protect themselves from predators.
5. Detecting sounds and smells that humans can't, dogs frequently bark and growl in response to these stimuli.
6. Hoping that someone would return his lost kitty, the owner offered a reward.
7. The veterinarian prescribed rest and vitamins for the sled dog that was exhausted from the Iditarod.
8. Surviving harsh winters in the mud of a frozen pond, turtles efficiently use oxygen throughout the winter.
9. To discourage predators, garter snakes emit a malodorous, musky scent.
10. Aware that the earth has had periods of global warming and global cooling long before people existed, scientists encourage an awareness of history during debates about the role of human-caused climate change.

*Answers to question A vary

Exercise 2.7a: Comma Rules

1. #2
2. #1
3. #3

4. #4
5. #4
6. #1
7. #1
8. #2
9. #3
10. #5

Exercise 2.7b: Commas in Context

1. A
2. A
3. B
4. B
5. A
6. B
7. B
8. B
9. B
10. A

Exercise 2.7c: Semicolon Use

1. B
2. A
3. B
4. A
5. A
6. B
7. A
8. A
9. A
10. B

Exercise 2.7d: Colon Use

1. Colon after *reasons*
2. Colon after *conclusion*
3. Colon after *goal*
4. Colon after *quote*
5. Colon after *me*
6. Colon after *clearer*
7. Colon after *help*
8. Colon after *assignment*
9. Colon after *subject*
10. Colon after *quote*

Exercise 2.7e: Dashes and Parentheses

1. My sister—the kindest person I've ever met—said she's going to give me her old car when she buys a new one.
2. My brother (who also was born in July) wants to go to a Knicks game for our birthday.
3. If you really want to know how I feel about my mother (I hope you don't), ask me when I'm in a better mood.
4. Bring me a ratchet and a socket—the 12mm socket that's right there on the table.
5. She kept her promise (for the first time ever) to pay me back.
6. "Please don't go. Wait! Come ba—"
7. The team (which I don't root for by the way) appeared dejected after losing a fifth straight game.
8. The Desario family members are broke—they don't have a cent to their name.

9. When she returned my call (she said it took so long because she lost my number), she seemed to think I owed her something.
10. Thursdays—as I've told you many times—aren't good days for me to meet.

Exercise 2.7f: Apostrophe Use

1. plural
2. possessive; nose's
3. plural and possessive; dogs' bowls
4. plural
5. contraction; can't
6. plural and possessive; women's
7. possessive; Elaine's; possessive brother's
8. possessive; sport's
9. contraction; it's
10. contraction; You'll
11. possessive pronoun
12. plural
13. possessive pronoun
14. contraction; haven't
15. possessive; apostrophe's

Exercise 2.7g: More Apostrophes

1. A
2. B
3. A
4. C
5. B
6. A

7. B
8. A
9. C
10. B

Exercise 2.8a: Easily Confused Words

1. should've
2. might've
3. your
4. you're
5. except
6. accept
7. then
8. than
9. who
10. whom
11. that
12. who
13. threw out
14. Throughout
15. less; fewer
16. fewer
17. There;their
18. they're;there
19. lose
20. loose
21. principle
22. principal; principal; principles
23. it's
24. its
25. definitely

26. defiantly
27. between
28. among
29. affected
30. effect

Exercise 2.9a: Capitalizing Titles

1. B
2. B
3. A
4. B
5. B
6. B
7. B
8. B
9. A
10. A

Exercise 3.1a: Intro to Sentence and Paragraph Style

1A. beacon, light, seared, flames, daybreak
1B. shadow, night
1C. score, years, momentous, daybreak, end, long, night, one hundred years, later, still, today
1D. manacles of segregation, chains of discrimination, lonely island of poverty, corners of American society exile
2A. captivity—not free

2B. One hundred years later

2C. How much time has past but how little conditions have improved

3A. is, crippled, lives, languished, finds, dramatize

3B. manacles, segregation, chains, discrimination, island, poverty, ocean, corners, exile, land, condition = nouns. Adj = lonely, vast, shameful

3C. free and captive; light and dark; past and present; alone and together; poor and rich

* Answers will vary on the paragraph

Exercise 3.2a: Precision and Word Choice

1. frustrated
2. competent
3. amiable
4. an elegant
5. nauseated
6. anguished
7. accurate
8. forlorn
9. ecstatic
10. nostalgic

Exercise 3.2b: Word Choice

1. C
2. B
3. B

4. A
5. A
6. B
7. C
8. A
9. C
10. B

Exercise 3.3a: Word Choice

Answers may vary throughout this section since there are myriad ways of achieving concision.

1. Delete *when it's cold*
2. Delete *when it's cold* or
3. Delete *together*
4. Delete *is the reason*
5. Delete *of opinion*

Exercise 3.3b: More Concision

Answers may vary throughout this section since there are many ways of achieving concision.

1. If you forget to call, don't worry because I'll call you.
2. That A-Rod used steroids and lied about it should prevent him from entering the Hall of Fame.
3. Predictably, the New York Jets disappointed their fans.
4. Since you're a nice person, I would like to ask you to the prom.
5. Every day, they annoy me.

Exercise 3.3c: Concision through Combining

1. B
2. A
3. A
4. B
5. A

Exercise 3.4a: Varying Sentence Openings

Answers may vary throughout this section since there are myriad ways of achieving variety.

1. Speeding down the street, he lost control of his car.
2. Changing our opinion on the matter, we now believe that you are right.
3. Foolishly disregarding my professor's suggestions, I ended up failing the exam.
4. Brutally smashing the victim's skull, the thug was a man of no conscience.
5. Underneath the desk sticks dry, white gum.
6. In my backyard lurks an eerie old elm try.
7. The dingy motel has a putrid smell.
8. A filthy pigsty, this bedroom needs to be cleaned.
9. Driving so slowly down the street in his hybrid vehicle, he was even passed by kids on tricycles.
10. Knock-kneed and coughing like hags, we cursed as we marched through the sludge.

Exercise 3.4b: Variety via Coordinating Conjunctions

1. C
2. B

3. B
4. A
5. B
6. A
7. B
8. C
9. C
10. B

Exercise 3.4c: Variety via Subordinating Conjunctions

Answers may vary throughout this section since there are myriad ways of achieving variety.

1. After sprinting the entire way home, I passed out from exhaustion.
2. While Kitty Genovese pleaded for help, bystanders did nothing.
3. Although our pitcher gave up only one earned run, we still lost the game.
4. Because you didn't show any gratitude, they think you're rude.
5. Since Rick began racing competitively five years ago, he has won several medals.
6. Once my mother cleans the dishes, I will wipe the countertops.
7. After we ate dinner, we had dessert.
8. Even though you are funny and rich, I don't want to marry you.
9. Because my mother and father never saved a cent, they never had money for emergencies.
10. Although I love you very much, I don't love the way your breath smells at this moment.

Exercise 3.4d: Variety via Conjunctive Adverbs

Answers may vary throughout this section since there are myriad ways of achieving variety.

1. I should have stayed up late and finished my paper; instead, I watched Monday night football, gorged on hot wigs, and procrastinated on my Calculus homework.
2. You lied, you cheated, and you never said you're sorry; consequently, you no longer have a girlfriend.
3. On Thursdays, I usually study before going to the gym; however, today I went to Friendly's and skipped the gym.
4. For a year, I put ten dollars per paycheck into my saving; however, I still don't have enough money for hair transplants.
5. Jennifer showed up for class, submitted her work on time, and asked for help; therefore, she earned an A.
6. Richard attended every lecture, completed his work on time, and asked for help; however, he earned only a C+.
7. Although he is friendly, Dr. Jones is an incompetent professor; therefore, his students don't learn much from him.
8. Superintendents are highly paid and wield a lot of power; therefore, they must show personal and financial restraint.
9. Most students buy their textbooks online; however, I buy them directly from the bookstore
10. If you come too close, you may get burned; however, if you stay too far away, you may not be warmed by the heat.

Exercise 3.4e: Variety via Relative Pronouns

Answers may vary throughout this section since there are myriad ways of achieving variety.

1. The store, which sells everything you need, is not far from here.
2. The writer, who usually proofreads carefully, didn't revise for grammar.
3. Citi Field, which has a capacity of 45,000 people, opened in 2009.
4. The man, whose son is a fireman, perished in a fire.
5. Jennifer, who was exhausted and ill, showed up anyway and performed beautifully.
6. Michael, whose mother was a talented guitarist, is a versatile musician.
7. I bought a puppy for the woman whom I love.
8. I can't find the book that you lent to me yesterday.
9. We waited more than an hour for the advisor who was stuck in traffic on the Long Island Express way.
10. Last summer we vacationed in Nice, which is located in southern France on the Mediterranean Sea.

Exercise 3.5a: Identifying Active and Passive Voice

1. Active
2. Active
3. Passive
4. Passive
5. Passive

Exercise 3.5b: Voice in Context

Answers may vary throughout this section since there are myriad ways of converting to the voice indicated

1. The milk was spilled on the table.
2. Kennedy was assassinated by Oswald.
3. The director filmed the scene in black and white.
4. The president signed the bill.
5. Witnesses saw the suspect fleeing from the scene of the crime.

Exercise 3.5c: More Voice

Answers may vary throughout this section since there are many rationales. Try to include support from the rationales at the beginning of the section on voice.

1. A
2. B
3. B
4. A
5. B

Exercise 3.6a: Topic Sentences and Paragraph Unity

Answers show which supporting sentences should have been stricken because they don't relate.

1. A, D, F
2. B, C
3. D, F
4. B, E

Exercise 3.6b: Paragraph Unity

Answers show which supporting sentences should have been stricken because they don't relate.

Paragraph 1: 2, 5, 8
Paragraph 2: 3, 6
Paragraph 3: 1, 5, 6,
Paragraph 4: 3, 4, 5, 8
Paragraph 5: 5

Exercise 3.6c: Creating Paragraphs

Passage A
1. C
2. D

Passage B
1. B
2. A

Passage C
1. D
2. B

Passage D
1. D
2. D

Exercise 3.7a: Transitions between Sentences

1. D
2. A
3. C
4. B
5. C
6. A
7. A
8. D
9. B
10. B

Exercise 3.7b: Transitions between Paragraphs

1. A
2. B
3. A
4. B
5. B

Exercise 4.1a: Characteristics of Good Titles

1. C
2. B
3. A
4. B
5. C
6. A
7. C
8. B
9. A
10. C

Exercise 4.2a: Characteristics of Effective Openings

Assignment 1: B
Assignment 2: A
Assignment 3: B
Assignment 4: B

Exercise 4.3a: Qualities of a Good Ending

1. A
2. B
3. B
4. A or B are correct. Please be prepared to defend each choice.

Exercise 4.4a: Effective Thesis Statements

1. 1B
2. 2C
3. 3A
4. 4A
5. 5C
6. 6B
7. 7C
8. 8B
9. 9A
10. 10C

Exercise 5.1a: Using Supporting Quotes

Answers may vary throughout this section since there are myriad ways of fusing quotes with your words.

1. The three parts of the note-taking process are "observing, recording, and reviewing" (Ellis 149).
2. Washington's most important job was "to win the war" (Ellis 108).
3. One role of the jester is to "educate" people the way a "teacher" does (Sanders 78).
4. The mother wants to love her children, but there is a "hard little place" in her heart that prevents her from loving "anybody," including her children (Lawrence 1).

Exercise 5.2a: Using Parenthetical Citations

1. Correct
2. Incorrect. (Yeats 20).
3. Incorrect. (Jones 7).
4. Incorrect. (James 11, 12).
5. Incorrect. (Silverstein and Bowers 74).
6. Incorrect. (rdk.jones.van.com)
7. Incorrect. (Leviticus 9:2).
8. Incorrect. (Frey et al. 5).
9. Incorrect. (Shakespeare II.iv.126-131).
10. Correct

Exercise 5.3a: Title Format

1. Italicized
2. Quotes
3. Italicized
4. Quotes
5. Italicized
6. Italicized
7. Quotes

8. Italicized
9. Italicized
10. Italicized

Exercise 5.4a: Dialogue Writing

1. D
2. B
3. C
4. B
5. B
6. A
7. A
8. B
9. D
10. A
11.

NOTES

1. The information in this paragraph on Harbrace comes from Lunsford and Connors. "Frequency of Formal Errors in Current College Writing, or Ma and Pa Kettle Do Research. *College Composition and Communication.* Vol. 39, No. 4 (Dec., 1988), pp. 395-409. NCTE. JSTOR

CPSIA information can be obtained at www.ICGtesting.com
Printed in the USA
BVOW02s1940270916

463474BV00006B/12/P

9 781634 499934